Shepherd's Songbook

Shepherd's Songbook

for

Waldorf Schools, Grades 1, 2, 3

by

Elisabeth Lebret

Published by
Waldorf Publications
351 Fairview Avenue, Suite 625
Hudson, NY 12534

Reproduced and printed
with transfer of all reserved rights 2021
with permission from
Waldorf School Association of Ontario (WSAO),
9100 Bathurst Street #2
Thornhill, Ontario, Canada L4J 8C7

Original copyright 2004, 1975 Elisabeth Lebret
adopted by WSAO, 2016

Copyright 2023 Waldorf Publications
ISBN 978-1-943582-60-0
All rights reserved, including the right to reproduce this book or parts thereof in any form.

Credits:

Cover illustration by Thomas Dannenberg

Mayfest font (titles) by Thomas Dannenberg

Proofreading by Ruth Riegel

Author biographical notes by Jacob Cornelis

Design and author photo by Richard Chomko (Immedia)

Preface to the New Edition 2023

Shepherd's Songbook has been out of print for a while, and Waldorf Publications is thrilled and honored to be able to bring it back, a gift with permission from the Waldorf School Association of Ontario, available now for all to enjoy and use for learning.

* * *

Elisabeth Lebret spent her life devoted to music and, more specifically, to music done with children. She followed indications by Rudolf Steiner, philosopher, educator, artist, architect, agricultural guide, medical guide, and spiritual realist. Following these indications, Elisabeth Lebret plunged deeply into investigations of the different scales and the different moods of these scales. The "mood of the fifth," a mood that lives in the pentatonic scale most simply, was indicated as beneficial and accessible to young children. Coming from the world of the stars, hearing the harmony of the stars, little children delight in hearing this sound and mood reflected in the interval of the fifth in a pentatonic scale. They can also hear most easily high ranges in song and floating songs that tend never to feel ended.

This "mood of the fifth" is not so easy for adults to hear and understand. Elisabeth Lebret explored the meaning of this early childhood ability to hear and sing songs in this extraordinary scale and then find those songs that express this mood. She wrote hundreds of songs in the pentatonic scale and hundreds of songs that evoke the mood of the fifth. Through this work, she has helped countless Waldorf teachers to find this mood and to teach this pentatonic music. This music, in turn, has delighted countless children in Waldorf schools and beyond and to be lifted with these songs into the world aligned with the harmony of the stars as can be attained here on earth.

Shepherd's Songbook is a rich selection of these songs to sing and to play on pentatonic flutes or recorders, that carries children from the mood of the fifth in first grade through to the slightly more ordinary interval of the fifth in songs and on into a folk song mode, but still retaining some of the more ephemeral characteristics of this lilting "mood of the fifth." Some songs have a whole story in them—a gift to children, parents, and teachers. Whole fables are told in song and can then be used to act out these riveting tales of the foibles of animals (many of them who live in all of us!) in little dramas in the classroom or at home. Other songs engage children in using flutes and percussion instruments to enhance a song—delightfully challenging tasks for second graders! Secrets that live in these songs include the learning of rhythms and different meters and the combining of a voice with a music tool, all without having to "teach" these things out loud. These lessons live in the music ingeniously wrought to hold all this magic.

There are helping songs of the same kind for third graders as well. These continue the process of leading children more fully into this life we love here, past the time of starry memories. By third grade, understanding a more familiar diatonic scale (*do, re, mi, fa,* etc.)—being able to sing it and hear it and play it on a flute or a recorder—becomes the most helpful to a child's development and for a child's learning of how to hear, sing, and make music.

Readers will experience Elisabeth Lebret's marvelous, twinkling approach to the lyrics in songs that she matches with equally twinkling tunes. Her sense of the different moods of songs is breathtaking, and these move from reverence for the beauty of nature and the marvels of the world, to somewhat sad or to downright funny. An example? "The cuckoo and the donkey on one point disagreed; Who was the best in singing? Whose voice was best indeed?" The song ends with a competition between "Hee haw," and "Cuckoo, cuckoo," both pretty toneless—and loud!

* * *

We hope you will enjoy this book as much as we have. Whatever you do, for your children's sakes if not for your own, keep singing!

– Patrice Maynard
for Waldorf Publications

Preface to the 2004 Edition

The *Shepherd's Songbook* book was born out of the real-life needs of the author's daughter-in-law, Elisabeth Koekebakker, who teaches music at the Toronto Waldorf School. Elisabeth remembers how, back in the early days of the school (1970s), she would ask Alan Howard, the school's master teacher and mentor, to write a poem for a Grade Two saints block and how she would then take the poem to "oma," Elisabeth Lebret, and ask her to compose suitable music to go with the words.

Over time, these pieces of music were gathered together, along with many others which Elisabeth Lebret had known, loved, and translated. Elisabeth Lebret had taught music in Waldorf schools in the Netherlands and had a wealth of experience and culture on which to draw. Eventually the book took on a life of its own and grew into much more than a collection of music and songs that can be taught in Waldorf schools. It became a hands-on course in why things are done the way they are in Waldorf music education—for example: why pentatonic songs for the young child, why certain intervals at certain ages, how to introduce notes and rhythm. As well, this is one of the few books in existence that can help the teacher to develop a deeper understanding of how different forms of music resonate with the evolving consciousness of the growing child. This is the kind of knowledge that can serve to make the classroom experience more meaningful and profound for both teacher and students.

Since it was first published in 1975, Elisabeth Lebret's *Shepherd's Songbook* has become an integral part of Waldorf school music education in the primary grades. The four thousand copies already in circulation are used regularly as resource material in Canada, the United States, Mexico, Brazil, Argentina, Australia, New Zealand, Nepal, Japan, Romania, the United Kingdom, and throughout Europe. It's no exaggeration to say that this book has been woven into the very life of the Waldorf school movement and has become an integral part of what Waldorf education is today.

So, in the spring of 2003, when the third printing was dwindling, and the printer could not find the original plates, we took a hard look at the typewritten text and the hand-drawn music and decided that it was time to re-issue the book in a more up-to-date and accessible format, in part as a way of honouring the contribution which the book and its author have made to Waldorf music education. As this new edition is going to press in the summer of 2004, the author Elisabeth Lebret, at the age of 96, is still very much alive, alert and living an independent life at the Hesperus Fellowship Community, where she has lived since 1987.

We would like to acknowledge that the *Shepherd's Songbook* has not only been a gift to Waldorf education and Waldorf teachers around the world, but it has also been a gift to the Waldorf School Association of Ontario, to which the author has generously donated all proceeds and revenues from its publication and sale.

– Richard Chomko
for the Waldorf School Association of Ontario

Acknowledgements

The author is grateful for the use of copyrighted material granted by the following authors, composers and publishers:

Wilhelm Dörffler for "Ohne Zahl" from *Jung Horand*, private edition, Dornach, Switzerland.

Alan Howard for the text of "The Crow and the Fox," "The Tortoise and the Hare," and "The Stork and the Fox."

Freya Jaffke for "The Bread" from *Lieder in der Quintenstimmung*.

Aloys Künstler and Verlag das Seelenpflege Bedürftige Kind, Bingenheim, for permission to translate and reprint from *Das Brünnlein Singt und Saget*: "Fox, Fox!," "Evergrace," "Kettle Boil!," "Sun and Rain," "Sun Was Shining," "Song of Praise," "In the Name of the Lord," "Pussies on the Willow," and "The Moon."

Harriet Laurey and Uitgevery Holland for the text of "My Pony," "Cat and Mouse," and "The Werewolf," from *Alle Voetjes Dansen*.

Brigit Visser for the text of "Squirrel Nib Nab" ("Knibbeltje").

Lyn Willwerth for permission to use his translation of "The Moon" by Paula Dehmel, and "Pussies on the Willow" by Christian Morgenstern.

Hermien Yzerman for the text of "Shepherd's Breakfast," "April," "The Squirrel," "We Dwarfs," and "Spring Song" from *Bim, Bam, Belletje*.

Bärenreiter Verlag, Kassel, for "St. Martin" from Walther Hensel's *Heiligenlieder*.

Verlag Freies Geistesleben, Stuttgart, for the text of "Das Wilde Tier" from Kischnick's *Was die Kinder Spielen*.

Philosophisch-Anthroposophischer Verlag, Dornach, for "Auf der Erde steh' ich gern" from *Lieder für die Waldorfschule* by Paul Baumann.

B. Schott's Sönne, Mainz, for "Hiaderia" from *Der Fünfton*.

Uitgevery Servire, Wassenaar, Holland, for "Who Can Tell Me," "Ani Maämin," and "Kol Dodie" from Chaja Milner's *Het Jiddische Hart Zingt* and *Hoor de Stem van Mijn Beminde*.

Natura Verlag, Arlesheim, for the text of "All Things about Me" by Hans Pohl from Julia Bort's *Heilende Erziehung*.

McClelland and Stewart Ltd., Dodd, Mead and Comp., Inc, New York, S.S. Mullin, Fredericton, New Brunswick, for the text of "Winterstreams" by Bliss Carman.

The Forerunner Publications, Surrey, England, for the text of "The Watermill" from *Singing Words* by Molly de Havas.

Harald Lyche & Co, Drammen, Norway, for two songs from *Ga i Skoge* by Hans Børre Ørbaek.

Preface 1975

Haven't all teachers a little bit of a shepherd in them, especially in the lower grades? Whereas children in Waldorf schools have every opportunity to express themselves individually in pictures, in painting, in handwork etc., in music lessons they have to be part of the group, acting accordingly. It is the time element—having to start together, to stop together, to be (reasonably!) silent together in between songs or musical pieces—that makes the music lessons a special challenge to the teacher. Rudolf Steiner remarks that instrumental work in the lower grades is a question of authority, and what could be better than the shepherd's authority and the assistance of his ever-watchful dog Rover? They work together, seeing to it that every individual feels happy in the flock's activity. (See page 8)

Originally this book was written in Dutch as the result of quite a few years of teaching music in a Waldorf school in Holland. Its contents are meant to be a guide for those teachers who, apart from being a class teacher, teach music as well. If their task is lightened by the contents of this book, if it inspires them with new ideas for the building up of some little corner in the world of sound, it will have reached its goal.

The leading thoughts followed in the introductions and commentaries for each grade are drawn from Rudolf Steiner's indications for musical education, mostly to be found in the lectures published in the book *Art in the Light of Mystery Wisdom*. We have tried to link up with the major motives of the main lesson so as to bring musical material that may be a help or a support to the inner experience of those subjects.

The five-tone scale plays an important role, but apart from that also well-known folksongs have been included, mostly as material for recorder playing. (For reasons of copyright the texts of these folksongs could not be printed in this book.) Thus one-sidedness is avoided. The material for the recorder is, though unclassified, to be found between the singing material because what is played on the recorder should be sung first and be well known. Only then should it be played on an instrument. These offerings are marked with an asterisk.

Unless indicated otherwise, texts and music have been translated or written by the author.

I would like to thank all those who have assisted me in putting this book together in English. I am particularly indebted to Mel Belenson for his help in translating, typing, and correcting. I hope many teachers will be able to draw advantage from my experience, my little songs, and musical discoveries made throughout my years of teaching—advantage not only by direct use, but also by analogous investigations into the kingdom of sounding phantasy.

– *Elisabeth Lebret*

Introduction to Grade 1

In 1923 Rudolf Steiner gave two lectures to the teachers of the Waldorf School in Stuttgart and the students of the Eurythmy school: "The Human Being's Experience of Tone" (published in English in *Art in the Light of Mystery Wisdom*). When translated literally from the German, this title should be: "The Experience of Tone *in* the Human Being." And that is truly what the contents of these lectures are about, the fact that man and music are a unity and cannot be considered separately, with the development of music running parallel to that of the human being.

Hence we cannot enter a first-grade classroom and just sing there a nice children's song. We have to be aware of the stage of development first-grade children are in and put that knowledge into an adequate musical language. Here one might feel in an awkward position because we are all educated with some sort of music, according to our place of birth and experience that have conditioned us in body and soul. One really has to widen one's horizon in this respect, which might be difficult for many teachers.

In the lectures cited above, Rudolf Steiner states that the child, until his ninth year, lives in the mood of the fifth: "We may not want to acknowledge the fact, but the child still lives essentially in the mood of the fifth interval. Naturally for teaching purposes, compositions can be used which also contain intervals of a third. But if we really want to reach the child, the cultivation of his musical understanding must commence with an understanding of the fifth. This is the really important point. And then we can give great benefit to the child if we approach him with the major and minor moods ... when he has passed the ninth year... ." (*Art in the Light of Mystery Wisdom*, p. 127).

To be able to understand this statement, we will have to consider it in a wider perspective and place it in the whole of Rudolf Steiner's concept of the human being's experience of intervals. In the same lecture he speaks about the totally different experience of music by ancient mankind in far bygone times. Man in those times was not able to hear anything within such wide intervals as the seventh, the none, and even the decime. Moreover, hearing them, he was immediately lifted into the supersensible world with his consciousness. He could say equally well either: "I am experiencing music" or "I feel myself to be in the spiritual world."

Only very gradually, with man's descent into the physical body, did it become possible to hear music and at the same time not to lose oneself. For a long time, throughout millennia after the Flood, mankind took pleasure in experiencing the fifth, after the seventh "had become painful," as Rudolf Steiner expresses it. He was now so far descended that not only the fifth as such but also a sequence consisting of tones related to each other by the fifth was now generally experienced. We read: "For long ages during post-Atlantean times, a scala, elaborated according to our present tonal sequence would, for example, have been: $d - e - g - a - b$, and again $d - e$ (p.119). There would have been no f and no c. This scale, in notation, looks as follows :

Page 10

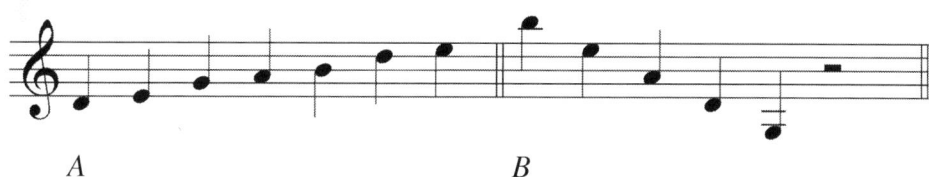

       A   *B*

A shows the sequence as it is mentioned, *B* shows the fifth's relations of which it has been formed. *A* shows the closed, *B* shows the outspread fan. *A* is the narrowed form of *B*. A good picture to show how the consciousness of the human being gradually descended, evaluating from airy forms to more solid ones!

Reconsider the sequence Rudolf Steiner suggested: Most of our intervals appear, with the exception of the major seventh and the minor second or semitone. Especially the lack of the latter gives to a pentatonic song that special flavour. Could it be that the child until his ninth year is not yet naturally inclined to that narrow interval? In music, the process of the descending ego into the physical body is expressed by a narrowing of the intervals mankind is able to experience. This process is repeated in the individual development of every human being; hence, we have to deal with it in education.

In his very valuable little book *The Development of Music in the Course of Development of Tone Systems* (*Die Entwicklung der Musik im Wandel der Tonsysteme*, Oda Verlag, Köln) Hans Erhard Lauer states that in many places in the world—where Greek thinking did not penetrate—five-tone music was preserved. Songs of the Hebrides, Irish and Scottish folksongs brought to the American continent by settlers (Appalachians, Nova Scotia), folksongs of Native Americans, from South America, from remote places in Eastern Europe, and many more places seem to confirm H.E. Lauer's statement. In all those places the mood of the fifth lived on, long after the musical development of the New Time took place in Western and Middle Europe.

Similarly, the young child might need some time to grow into later forms of music; he might need some remoteness to be able to develop his musical faculties in an adequate way. That nowadays he is surrounded by music that does not take this into consideration is not really the point. The point is that we, by Rudolf Steiner's indications, should now be able to observe how far a first-grade child is advanced in his musical development. His experience of the world is still very much in his environment … parents, brothers and sisters, teacher … they all are part of the child's "ego world" that is not yet an inner world. It is typical for first graders that they do not really want to end a song on the tonic, being the expression of the feeling that we live in a physical body *(p. 27)*. It is this growing feeling in the child that we have to deal with in the lower grades. In Grade 1 they are often quite happy to end a song on what we would feel would be the fifth or the third:

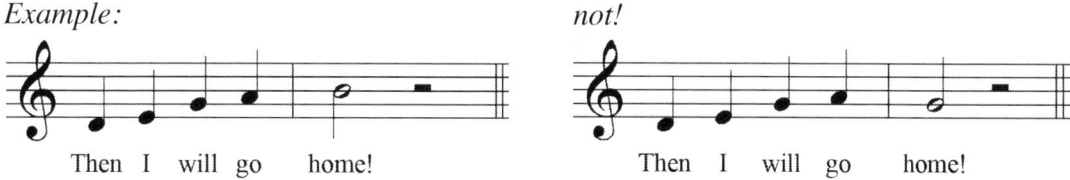

Page 11

Considering such things, one might make a very inconvenient discovery: In the light of the preceding thoughts, there are quite a few children's songs which one should drop or… change! For example the widespread nursery song about Briar Rose, "The princess was a lov'ly child" (*Dornröschen war ein Königskind*), emphasizes the tonic in a way that does not seem adequate in connection with a fairy tale!

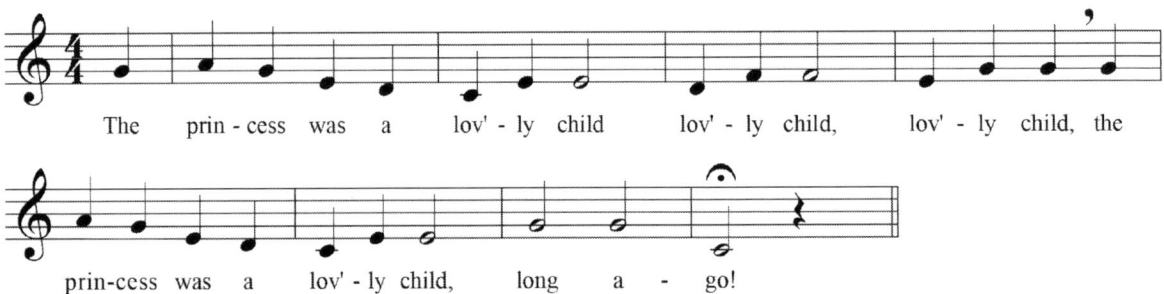

This could be changed into the sequence indicated by Rudolf Steiner:

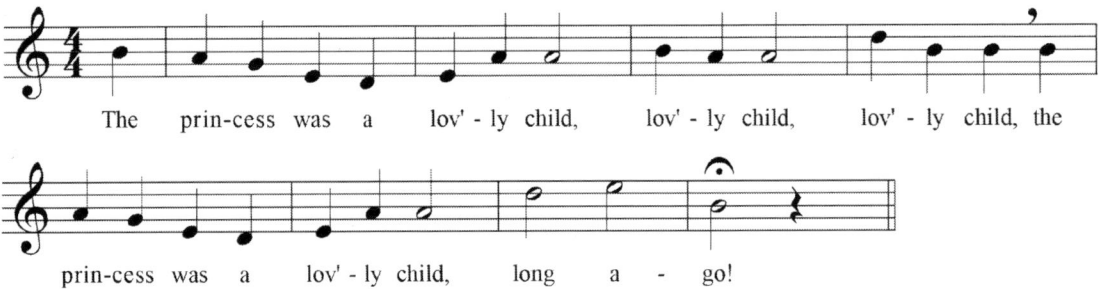

On the other hand, one one might find in Irish, Scottish, Canadian, and American songbooks the most beautiful pentatonic melodies, but with wholly unsuitable texts. For example:

Building a Slide

And there is a third category of songs that apparently are made up in a neat and pure five-tone scale, but they emphasize the tonic so strongly that they have lost the pentatonic character: "Old Mac Donald Had a Farm," and "The Farmer in the Dell" for example. All this beautiful pentatonic material is a remnant of bygone times, which in one way or another has grown with the consciousness of the people of its origin. For reasons just mentioned it cannot serve our need of five-tone songs for Grades 1 and 2. However we should not forget or ignore the influence of the sound children are exposed to nowadays. Therefore, in our attitude we should try to reconcile the contradiction as much as possible.

If we use five-tone music—all right! But not fanatically, excluding all other sound. That is why in this book one will find other material as well.

The following songs for Grade 1 do not seem to have any apparent connection to each other; however, in the course of practical work they are held together by a story which, throughout the seasons, is told during the music lessons. The story creates a similar atmosphere to that of the main lesson (fairy tales!). The pictures of the story lead quite naturally to the little songs Rudolf Steiner prescribed for Grade 1 (*The Kingdom of Childhood*, Torquay, 1924, p. 112), singing little songs, but they should be well sung! The songs are made up or found in connection with the story of a shepherd living in a little house near the "woodland meadow." His life with the flock and with Rover, the dog, is the subject of an endless narrative to which every week some small thing is added. Rickydouse, the goblin, the shepherd's grandson visiting his grandfather every week, and many other side-motifs, partly drawn from suitable little songs, keep up the attention.

In this way, along with the pictures, a healthy balance between listening and inner experience on one hand and singing and playing on the other can be established. The mood we are in during the experience of sound is of the utmost importance. We should not try to impart faculties right away; those have to develop "as by themselves" over time. And they do!

In the same way the instrumental part of the music lesson can be handled. As Rudolf Steiner recommended a blowing instrument, most of the Waldorf schools use soprano recorders tuned in C. Played by six-year-olds they do not naturally produce the nicest sound, but they have the advantage that they can be used for pentatonic songs as well as for songs in the C major scale. If only one golden rule could be followed by teachers—namely that playing loudly should be prevented from the very first moment—the result can be quite satisfactory.

This can be handled in the following way: Among the material for Grade 1, one will find a little song which has been called "Gate into Recorder Playing." This is the very simplest song —one could even call it a "sing-song"—meant to wrap, as it were, the children's consciousness in that special mood of listening, and at the same time appeal to their natural capacity for imitation. The child is simply shown what he has to do. This saves a lot of explanation about left and right, names of fingers and the like. First graders really do not yet know their "body geography."

The last two lines of the song are meant to be played, but at first they should be sung for some time, being an exercise for "tonguing." Not until every child has his left hand on top of the recorder (and nobody is squeaking on his own!) has the great moment come for playing the "doo" tone together! In the case of a soprano recorder, this has to be the *b*.

In this way the instrumental part of the music lesson, which, according to Rudolf Steiner, is just a question of authority, is made into a social happening right away! Everything that is going to be played should be sung first and well known. The reason for this is that **the finger movements should operate on hearing**, the visual help we give as the teacher on our recorder being only a support. That is why the material for recorder playing should be of the utmost simplicity: A two-tone song in Grade 1 can cause deepest satisfaction when the children hear that they produce a beautiful sound. Let us see to it that our students listen actively, as a counterbalance to all those sounds they are surrounded by and exposed to during daily life.

Our way of teaching music is not meant to restrain the child's musical development, but to let him, as it were, gently down as on a parachute. As a result, toward his ninth year, he might be properly prepared to find his own basic tone or tonic as the expression of his deepest being.

✻ ✻ ✻

Rudolf Steiner gives us a keynote on how to deal in the music lessons with the soul-elements thinking, feeling, and willing (*Art in the Light of Mystery Wisdom*, p136f). The unprepared teacher can very easily land into unpleasant situations if he has no idea how to handle thinking, feeling, and willing in music. In this lecture we are given a clear concept of the relation between the soul-elements, represented in music by melody, harmony, and rhythm.

"The peculiarity of music is that it should neither ascend completely into the realm of ideas, nor should it descend entirely into the realm of will."

This means that we constantly have to seek a balance between thinking and willing, between melody and rhythm. Melody should not ascend into the world of concepts; rhythm should not "drown" in the element of will. The feeling element, being the heart of the matter, should balance between dream and activity. We recommend studying these ideas very carefully; they might prevent a lot of difficulties.

The Shepherd

This song creates that peaceful, placid mood, sensitive to sound, that can serve as a starting point for other (very gradually!) more lively material. The melody nearly moves all along the pentatonic scale. The iambus of the 6/8 measure rock the will-impulses to sleep, but the faster rhythms in between just prevent this. Thus we enter the land of peace where the shepherd is living, far from the noise of the outer world. There we relate to nature, to the seasons, to plants and animals. In this way we lay a foundation for the inner experience of all that "sounds" in the world.

Shepherd's Breakfast

This song illustrates the way the shepherd usually starts his day: lighting the stove, cooking a porridge... For the teacher the song might be more difficult than for the children to whom the pentatonic sound is still natural; it might ask for some effort to really penetrate it with feeling. Of course we should stir the pot, using every opportunity to move while singing.

The Shepherd

A shep-herd was liv-ing all a-lone in the wood-land mead-ow. He tend-ed his flock with all the sheep, through-out light and shad-ow. His shep-herd pipe had so mild a sound, and Ro-ver the dog, kept a sharp look-out! In the wood-land mead-ow.

Shepherd's Breakfast

Text: Herman Ijzerman
Translation: E.L.

Chim-done! you smoke! Fi-re, we poke! Ket-tle you bring wa-ter to sing! Cook-ing a por-ridge de-li-cious-ly hot! Cook-ing a por-ridge, while stir-ring the pot. Of milk and su-gar, of oats or of rye and the cin-na-mon add bye and bye! Por-ridge, por-ridge, please, now be done! Por-ridge, por-ridge, please now be done!

Fox, Fox!

From: *Das Brünnlein Singt und Saget*,
Aloys Künstler. Translation: E.L.

Fox, fox, just look out! I love my chick-ens there's no doubt! You took me one and got a-way! That's what the hun-ter will make you pay!

Page 15

Gate into Recorder Playing

This little song might, in the long run, play quite an important role in the music lessons. If the text is not appropriate, then change it accordingly! The main point is it should indicate how the recorder should be held. The last line: "Singing doo-doo-doo" is an exercise for "tonguing" (using the tongue as in whispering the syllable "doo"). To start with, that line should be sung, and only after some time—depending on the group—it can be played. It may happen that a few times we have to put away the recorders even before using them because some children cannot wait and start to play on their own. But when, at the end of the song, we manage at last to play the "doo" line together, that is quite a happening!

Throughout the school year, this song can be used as an introduction into recorder playing. Especially repeated week after week, it strongly supports starting to play the recorder. No need to say that the "doo" line is meant to introduce new tones, one after the other.

The Flock

This is a narrative, meant to be listened to. The 6/8 measure produces a feeling for the peaceful swelling of the moving sheep. The group can sing the last line directly.

The Tones

This song is made up for the sound *ng*, having a therapeutic effect on nasal passages and sinus. A help in times of miserable colds! The real significance of this sound is described by two singers, whose books are mentioned below.

2. High from the Heavens
   Ning, nang, nong!
   Tones are coming,
   Ning, nang, nong!
   In the churches' bells they ring,
   Carried by the wind!
   Ning, nong, ning, nong!

3. Hearing them coming,
   Ning, nang, nong!
   They have us dreaming,
   Ning, nang, nong!
   Of sunshine and of light and warmth
   And of the Lord's own Hand…
   Ning, nong, ning, nong!

Valborg Svadstrom-Werbeck: *Die Schule der Stimm-Enthüllung*.
Philosophisch-Anthroposophischer Verlag, Dornach, Switzerland.

Maria Führmann: *Die Praxis des Gesanges*.
Verlag die Kommenden, Freiburg i. Breisgau, Germany.

✱ Gate into Recorder Playing

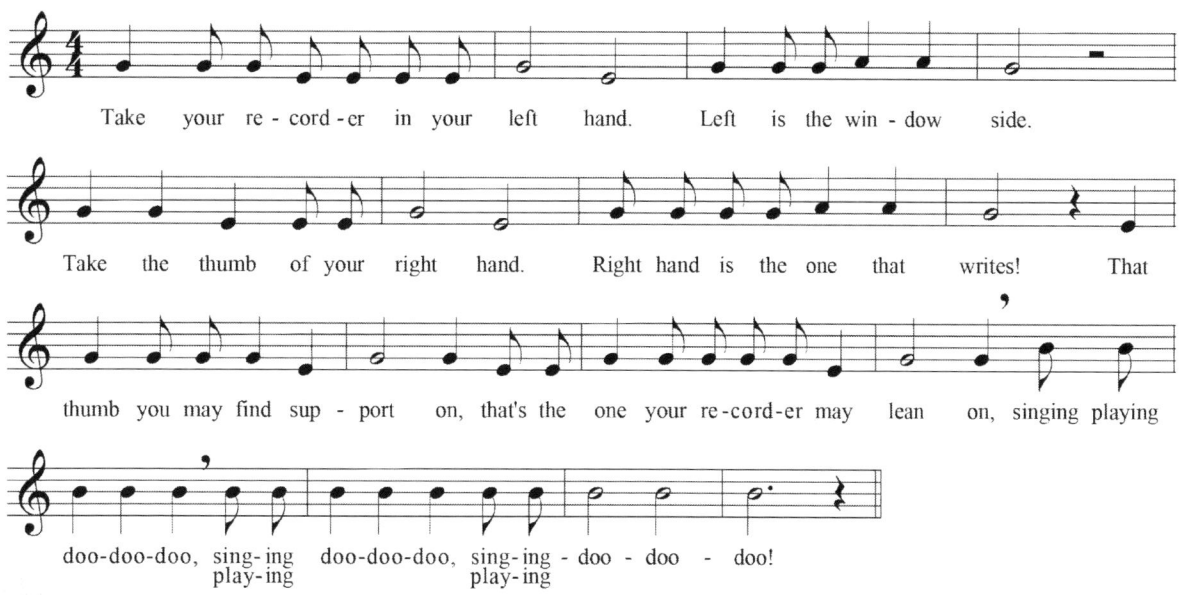

The Flock

The Tones

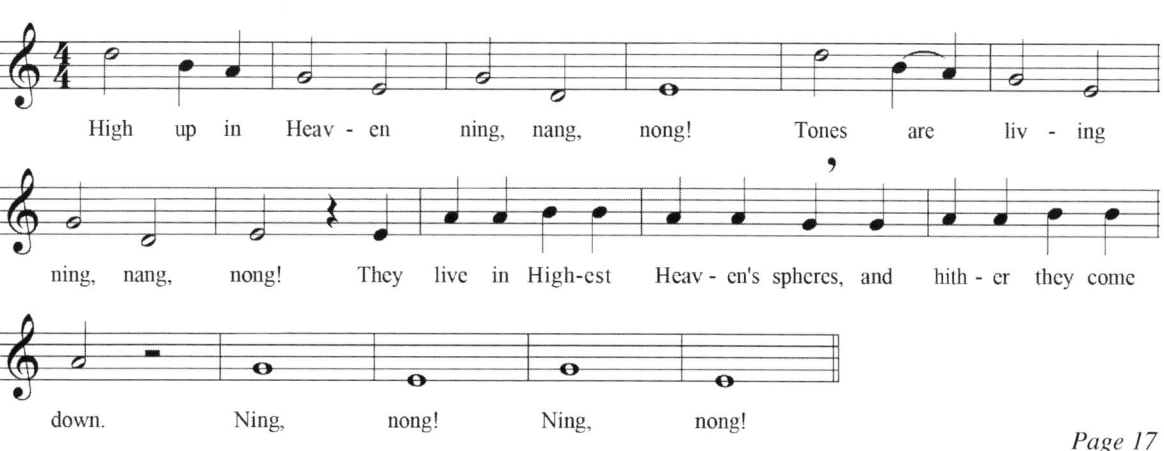

The Werewolf

Let's investigate how far we are able to handle the willing element in our group! For this the song of "The Werewolf" might serve us. After all, commotion should be there sometimes! One should take good notice of the two trochee, alternated by one dactyl; those should be sung very accurately, otherwise the song loses its form and will become a chaos!

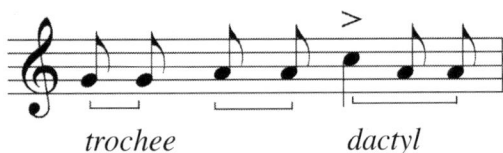

trochee   *dactyl*

The Squirrel

"The Squirrel" opens the opportunity to introduce a soloist. Whether acting and singing or only singing depends on the available talent. The little animal might act out his sprightliness on the dotted notes, expressing the nibbling, the finding of acorns, etc. If the space in the classroom allows it, it is recommended to have the whole group moving on the song's rhythm. Later, when learning notation, the experience of the dotted note (of which musical education mostly makes an arithmetical problem: "A dot after any note increases its length by one-half") in the limbs will be of some service at that time.

The Werewolf

Holland Publishers
Haarlem, Holland

Text: Harriet Laurey
from *Alle Voetjes Dansen*

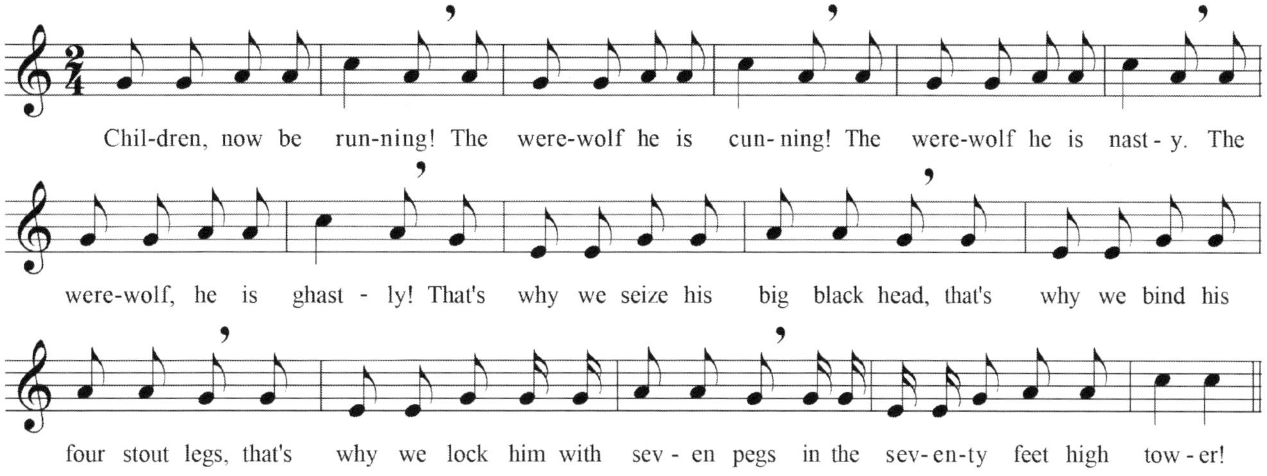

Chil-dren, now be run-ning! The were-wolf he is cun-ning! The were-wolf he is nast-y. The were-wolf, he is ghast-ly! That's why we seize his big black head, that's why we bind his four stout legs, that's why we lock him with sev-en pegs in the sev-en-ty feet high tow-er!

The Squirrel

Text: Hermien Ijzerman
Translation: E.L.

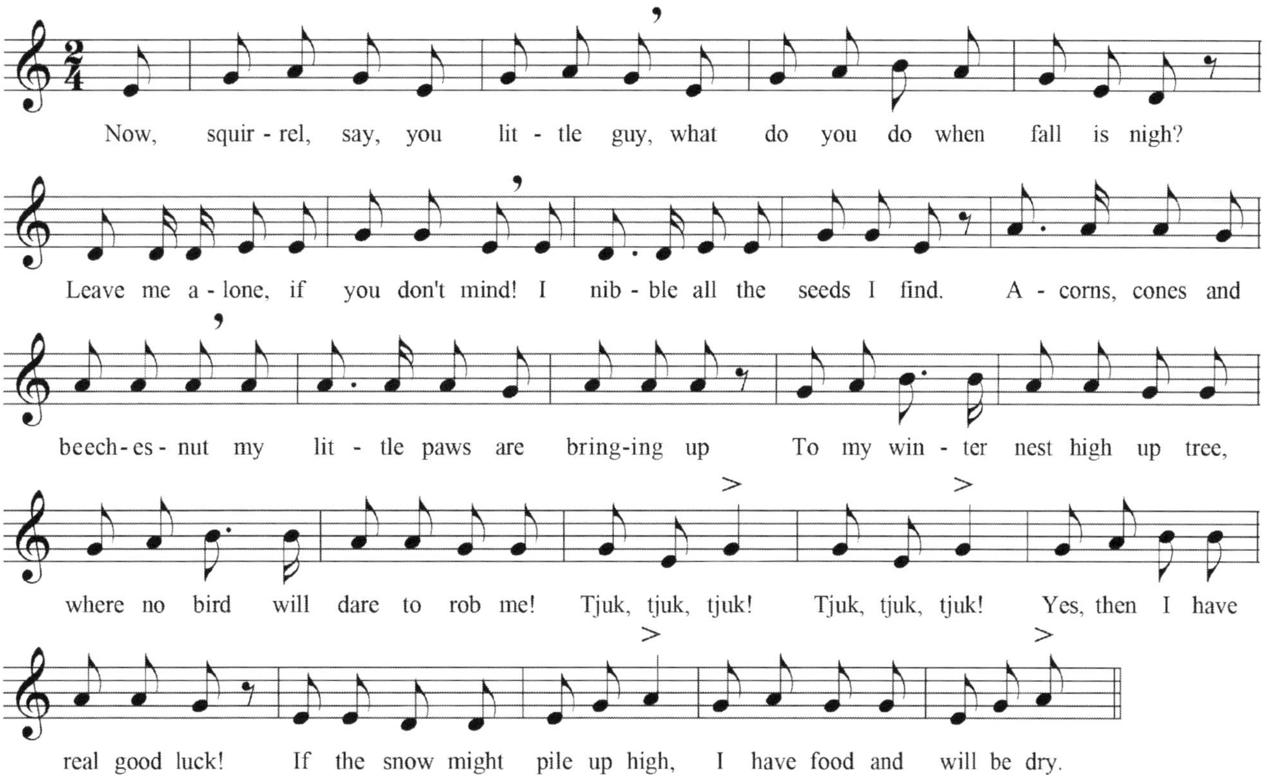

Now, squir-rel, say, you lit-tle guy, what do you do when fall is nigh? Leave me a-lone, if you don't mind! I nib-ble all the seeds I find. A-corns, cones and beech-es-nut my lit-tle paws are bring-ing up To my win-ter nest high up tree, where no bird will dare to rob me! Tjuk, tjuk, tjuk! Tjuk, tjuk, tjuk! Yes, then I have real good luck! If the snow might pile up high, I have food and will be dry.

Rickydouse

Rickydouse introduces himself to the shepherd's grandson and invites him to his house. In order to be small enough to enter the dwarf's living-quarters, he has to be touched by a magic wand! And now he is able to witness the dwarf's activities!

The first song is an exercise for recorder, especially for the tones e and d, played with the right-hand fingers. When singing it, the "doodle-deedle-doo" should be tapped on the table with the forefingers, the "rom-bom-bom" with the fists, and that should happen exactly in time! The basic tone c as the tonic, does not occur in the song; however inwardly, latently in the background it can be well perceived.

The second song is for play-acting. The tonic at the end of the first sentence expresses a feeling of well-being, caused by the performance of the different tasks. The rhythm should be very correct and alert; rhythm and action go hand in hand!

✱ Rickydouse

We Dwarfs Are Working Happily

Text: Hermien Ijzerman
Translation: E.L.

2. We dwarfs are working happily
   In the woodshed, in the woodshed.
   We dwarfs are working happily
   In the woodshed we like to be!
   We chop the wood, we chop the wood,
   We chop the wood, ho, hay!
   We chop the wood, we chop the wood
   That will burn in the stove one day!

3. We dwarfs are working happily
   in the cottage, in the cottage.
   We dwarfs are working happily
   In the cottage we like to be!
   We sweep the floor, we sweep the floor,
   We sweep the floor, you see!
   We sweep the floor, we sweep the floor,
   Spotlessly clean we may be!

4. We dwarfs are working happily
   In the kitchen, in the kitchen.
   We dwarfs are working happily
   In the kitchen we like to be!
   We stir the pot, we stir the pot,
   We stir the pot, ho, hay!
   We stir the pot, we stir the pot
   For the best meal of the day!

5. We dwarfs now want to go to bed
   In our bedroom, in our bedroom.
   We dwarfs now want to go to bed;
   We are tired, and all has been said.
   Sooja doo, sooja doo,
   Sooja doo, ho, hay!
   Sooja doo, sooja doo,
   And we dream of the bygone day!

March Wind

This song is consequently built on the metre of its text: an iambus followed by an anapest expressing the strength of the March wind. Clapping the rhythm is recommended. Also several smaller groups could alternate telling each other, by singing as well as clapping, what the March wind does. This would prevent an occasional disinterest, as an ongoing rhythm, without interruption, undoubtedly has a slackening effect on a group.

The Song of Four Seasons

This is a disguised exercise for recorder playing, for the moment when the children are able to play downward to d. In whatever season this is the case does not matter; the text provides for any time. Five times we play downward, three times up and down, with an end going up to b. One could easily make an end on g, which for us would sound like the tonic, but the children are entirely satisfied with the floating end. (See example in the introduction for Grade 1.)

Spring

Lovely, lovely springtime, with a wreath of light!
With a crown of yellow, yellow daffodils,
With a collar of pink and purple tulip frills,
Will you come all right?
Sure I'm on my way now, on a beam of light.
Winter has to go now, winter has had its time!
Let's now put some snowdrops all around;
Let's now charm the crocus from the ground.
Winter has to go!

Summer

Lovely, lovely summer, with your colours bright,
With a crown of airy, airy butterflies,
With a collar of blue and purple pansy-eyes,
Will you come all right?
Maybe, just a second, just a little while,
Spring should now be leaving, spring has had its time!
Let's start charming roses from the ground;
Let's spread lovely flowers all around.
Spring has now to go!

Autumn

Dear delightful autumn, with your splendid leaves,
With your red and brown and vivid yellow spell,
With your pears and apples all too good to smell,
Will you stay on long?
I do feel like staying on till Christmas–night,
Till the Holy Childe softly has arrived.
Until then I'll hang some fog around,
I'll be splashing rain upon the ground,
Before winter night.

March Wind

Text: Maud Uschold
from "Year around"

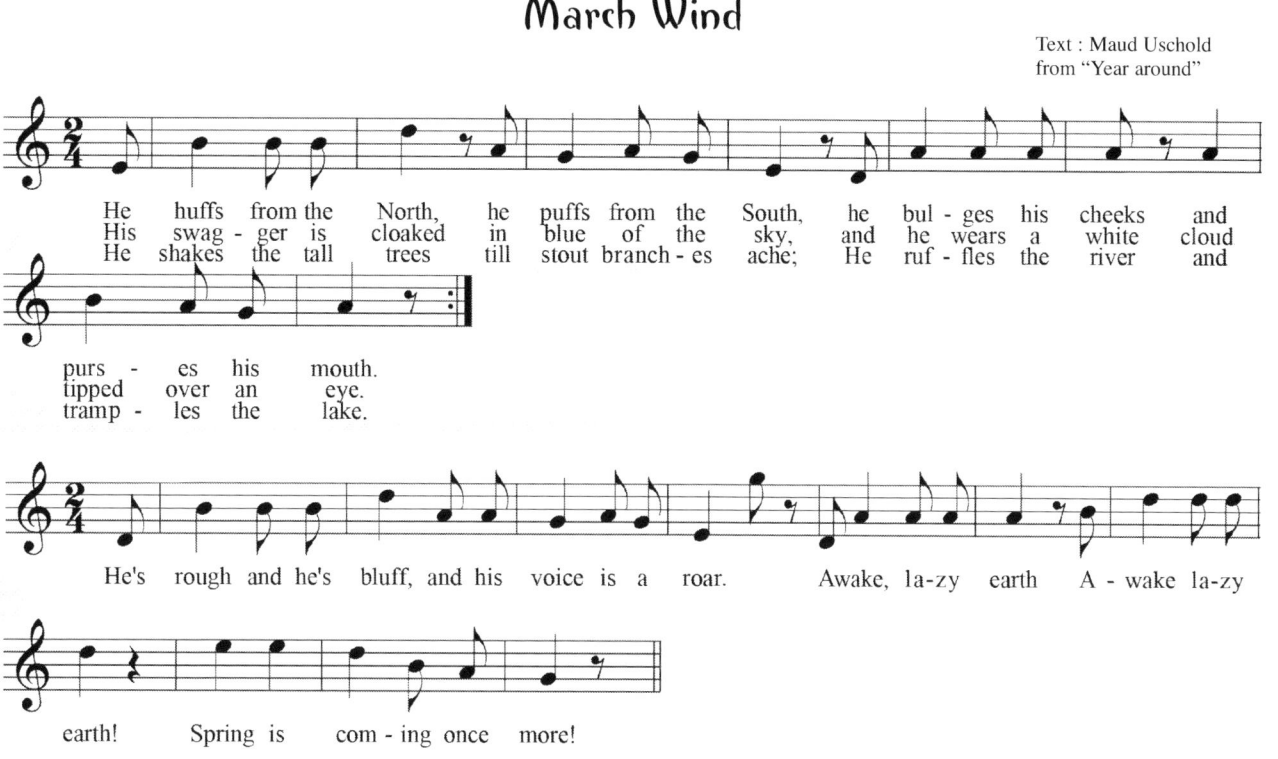

He huffs from the North, he puffs from the South, he bul-ges his cheeks and purs - es his mouth.
His swag-ger is cloaked in blue of the sky, and he wears a white cloud tipped over an eye.
He shakes the tall trees till stout branch-es ache; He ruf-fles the river and tramp-les the lake.

He's rough and he's bluff, and his voice is a roar. Awake, la-zy earth A-wake la-zy earth! Spring is com-ing once more!

✻ The Song of Four Seasons

Frost-y, frost-y win-ter, with a beard of fog, with a coat of soft and fur-ry po-lar-bear with a cap of wool-ly, wool-ly pus-sy-hair, when will you be off? In a few weeks' time now, sure I will be gone! In the cold-est North-land, I'll be all a-lone! I'm still throw-ing snow-flakes all a-round, I'm still fling-ing sleet up-on the ground, then I will go home.

My Pony

Again a song bringing some commotion! It is not linked to any season, thus can be used any moment we have to arrest the children's attention. We might start our story as suddenly as the pony himself appears galloping on the "woodland meadow": Where does he come from? To whom does he belong? (Which choleric child would like to have a good gallop in the classroom?) If we would try to find the tonic in this song, it would be *f*. It is built on the pentatonic sequence: $c - d - f - g - a - c$. We, as adults, can be well aware of *f* as the tonic, even if it does not sound as such. And it doesn't; none of the phrases end on it, not even the last one. In this way the tonic can be evaded, hidden, handled in a way so that its effect is not too strong.

Three French Two-Tone Songs

These little songs might serve for recorder playing the moment *a* and *b* can be played reasonably. The teacher should sing them, demonstrating the finger movements on the recorder. The main point is the beautiful regular rhythm of the songs, making the finger movements utterly simple. Of course the songs can also be played in other two-tone combinations.

Sun Was Shining

A delicious narrative, giving ample opportunity for play-acting. The melody, along the pentatonic line, turns around the *b* in the first phrase, then descends to the lower region where the sun sets and a sleeping mood sets in, in which the chorus is repeated. This chorus could also be played on the recorder, as it moves gently down and up again "along the line."

2. Tree was rust'ling all day long and says: "What could that be?
   When the sun has ceased to shine, then I can go to sleep!"

3. Bird was singing all day long and says: "What could that be?
   When the tree has ceased to rustle, I can go to sleep!"

4. Bunnies, pricking their long ears, they say: "What could that be?
   When the birds have ceased to sing, then we can go to sleep!"

5. Hunter stops to blow his horn and says: "What could that be?
   When there are no bunnies running, I can go to sleep!"

Evergrace and Kettle, Boil!

Two beautiful specimens of short and simple songs, full of humour! After they have been sung and well memorized, they can be played on the recorder. "Evergrace" is an exercise for playing the fifth *d – a*, for which one has to move four fingers at a time. Do not forget to introduce Evergrace in your story!

✱ Kettle, Boil!

Page 26

Sun Was Shining

From *Das Brünnlein Singt und Saget*
Aloys Künstler. Translation: E.L.

Sun was shin-ing all day long and says: "Now let it be!" Goes to bed and shuts his eyes and gent-ly falls a-sleep. — Doo! doo! doo! And like-wise does my lit-tle child be-cause it's sleep-y too! Then the moon is look-ing down-ward, says: "What could that be? No hun-ter blow-ing? No bun-nies run-ning? No bird-ies sing-ing? No trees are rust-ling? No sun is shin-ing? And child a-lone would be a-wake? No! no! no! The lit-tle child should go to sleep and shut his eyes just so!

✻ Evergrace

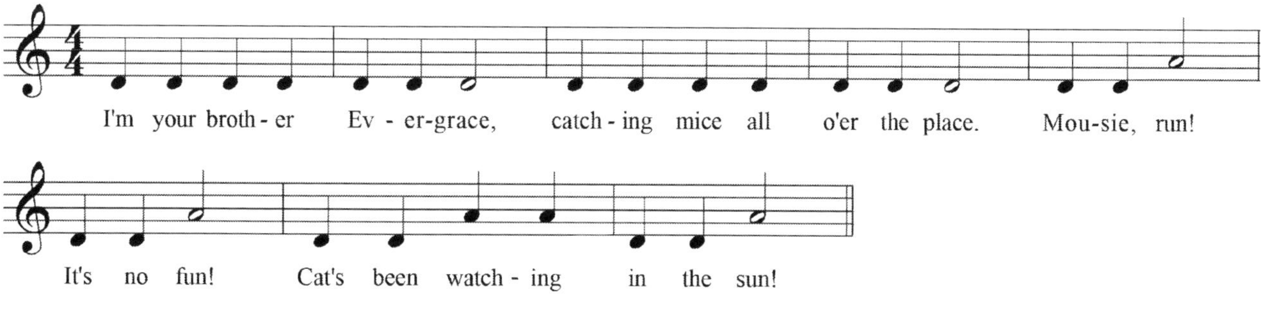

I'm your broth-er Ev-er-grace, catch-ing mice all o'er the place. Mou-sie, run! It's no fun! Cat's been watch-ing in the sun!

Thawing

This song has been specially made for recorder playing. As a matter of course, it should be sung first and well known by heart. It is recommended to prepare for playing by clapping the rhythm first, to have it penetrate thoroughly. Then the children will succeed better in "tonguing" the fast notes correctly. The specific exercise, however, consists of making the step from *g* down to *d*, for which three holes have to be covered. In "Evergrace," the fifth, for which four fingers have to move, has already been practised, but here the step from *g* to *d* occurs in combination with other steps, unexpectedly in the course of the song. It might seem only a trifle, but this again is a little step on the difficult path of recorder playing.

From: *Das Brünnlein Singt und Saget*
Aloys Künstler. Translation: E.L.

Sun and Rain

This is a very easy song, just to be sung in a lost moment; later it might be played as well. With such a little song, the children start to gradually experience that they are already able to produce some nice things on the recorder! Let them learn to play by heart, to cultivate their inner hearing!

From: *Das Brünnlein Singt und Saget*
Aloys Künstler. Translation: E.L.

Cat and Mouse

A narrative in the pentatonic sphere. Only one phrase ends on the tonic, that is, where it states: "You are not as smart as I am!" The melody is just running along "the line" and that is why it can be played on the recorder also. One has to add—or take away—only one finger at a time, with the exception of the ascending fifth at the end, but that might have been practised already in "Evergrace."

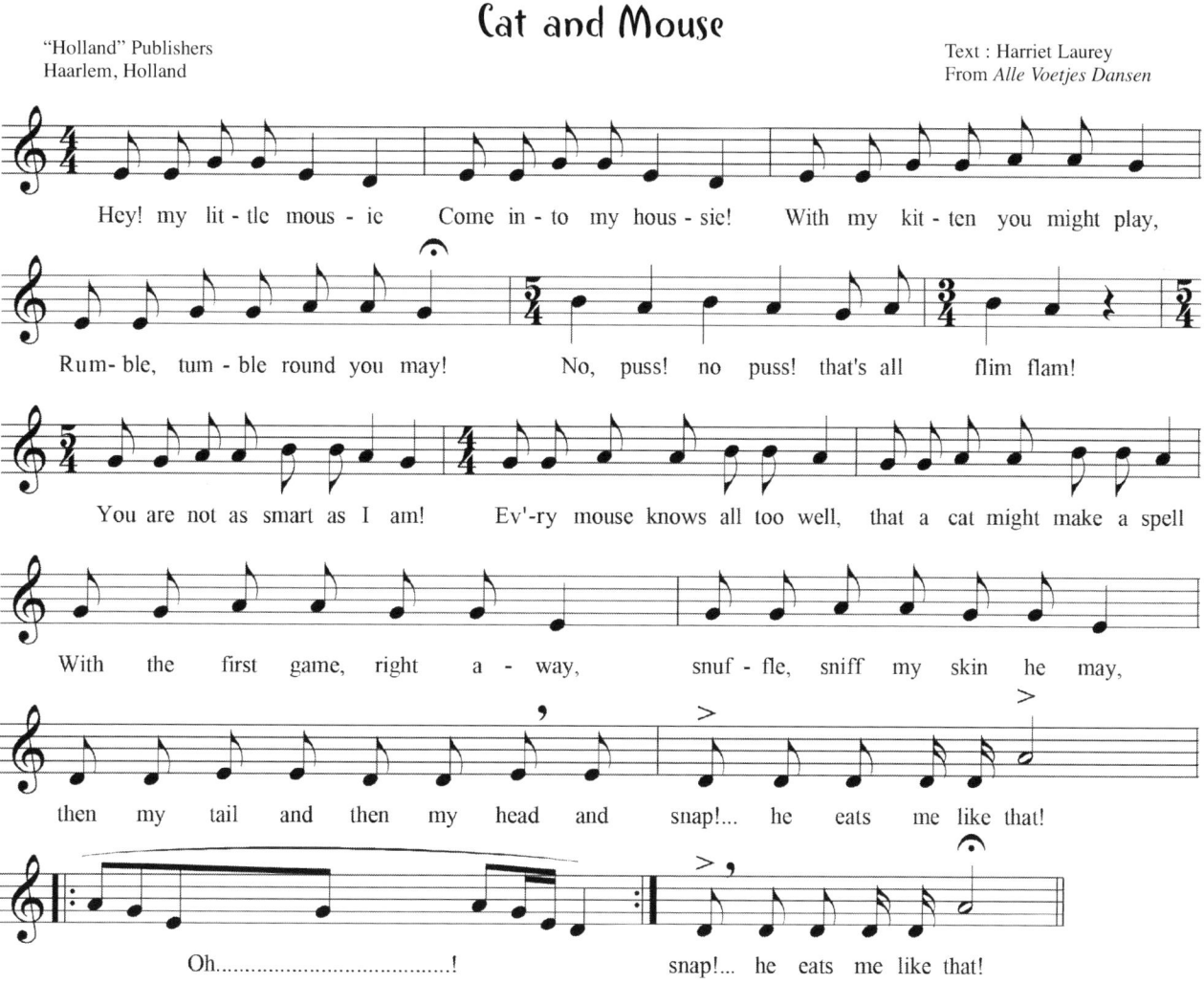

Christmas Song

Although the pentatonic scale does not express the Christmas mood very well (being the expression of musicality in pre-Cristian times), this text, musing as it does on an outer situation, lends itself very well to a five-tone song. During Advent time it might create a mood of anticipation.

Epiphany Song

This song presents an opportunity to play-act, the scene being set by the sleeping Joseph and Mary, the angel coming in and awakening them, etc. The ascending minor third of "Wake up!" has an evocative quality one should be well aware of. The last line should be sung by the whole group as they accompany Mary on her way to Egypt.

Quiet, Quiet!

This little Christmas song can be used as an opening for all sorts of Christmas activities. It is built on the descending minor third, an interval full of secret life when descending from the fifth of a scale. The c that would be the tonic here can be quite clearly perceived by inner hearing, but it does not once occur, not even at the end! The interval $e - f$, being a semitone, has a narrowing influence that takes away the pentatonic mood, but at the same time evokes an inner life which just seems to belong to Christmas time.

   2. Sheep on the hillside lay, whiter than snow,
      Shepherds were watching them, long, long ago!

   3. Then from a happy sky angels bent low,
      Singing their songs of joy, long, long ago!

   4. For in a manger bed, cradled, we know
      Christ came to Bethlehem, long, long ago!

Christmas Song

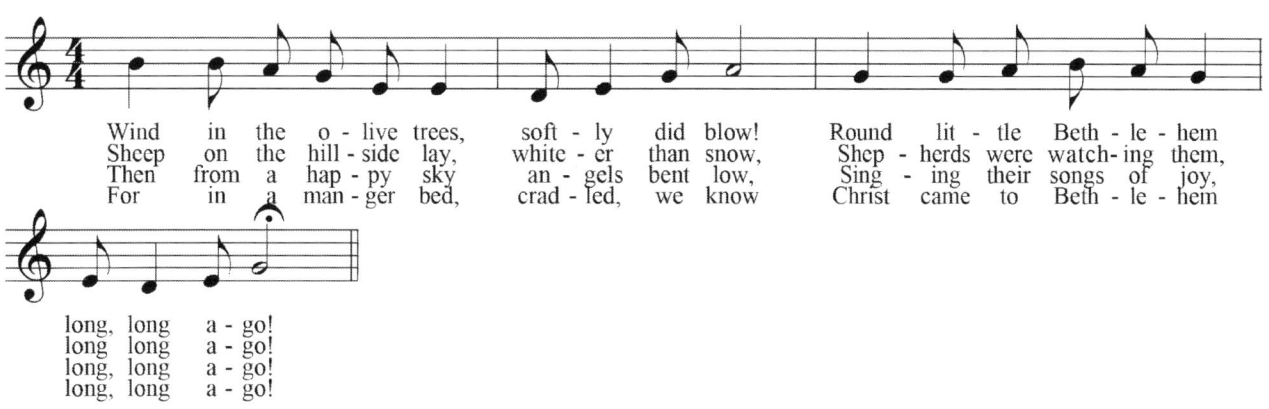

Wind in the o-live trees, soft-ly did blow! Round lit-tle Beth-le-hem
Sheep on the hill-side lay, whit-er than snow, Shep-herds were watch-ing them,
Then from a hap-py sky an-gels bent low, Sing-ing their songs of joy,
For in a man-ger bed, crad-led, we know Christ came to Beth-le-hem

long, long a-go!
long, long a-go!
long, long a-go!
long, long a-go!

Epiphany Song

Dutch Folksong

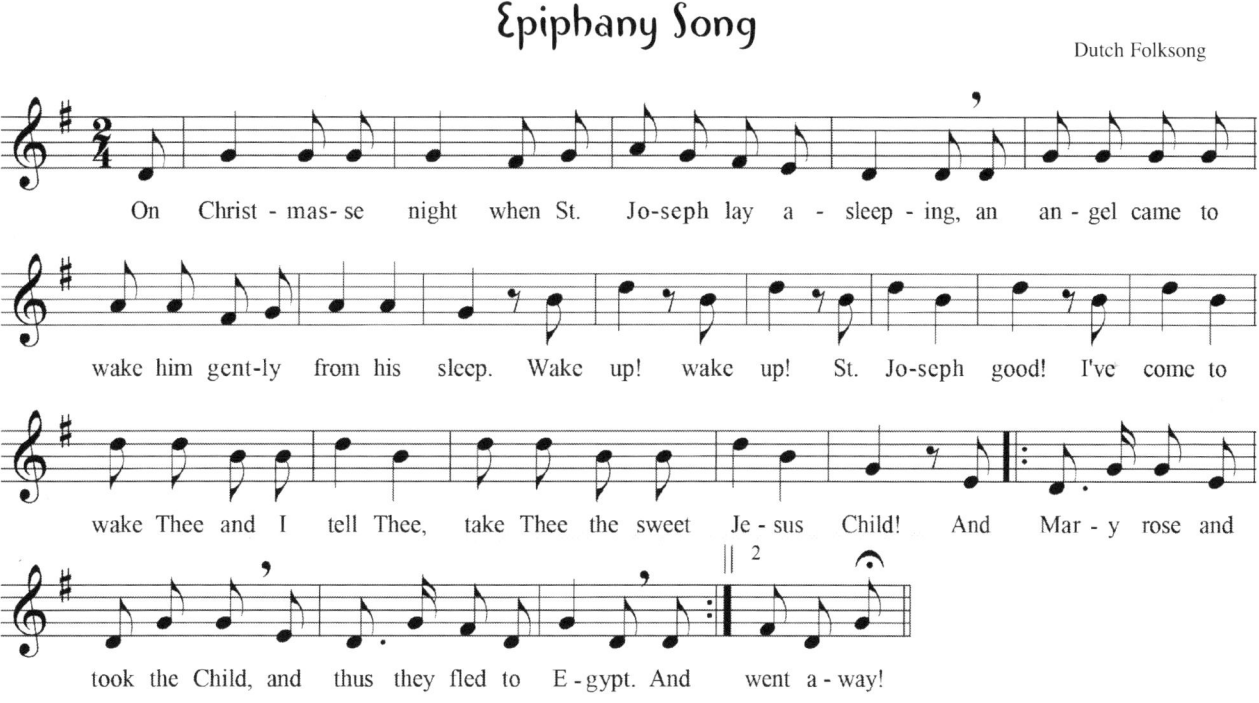

On Christ-mas-se night when St. Jo-seph lay a-sleep-ing, an an-gel came to wake him gent-ly from his sleep. Wake up! wake up! St. Jo-seph good! I've come to wake Thee and I tell Thee, take Thee the sweet Je-sus Child! And Mar-y rose and took the Child, and thus they fled to E-gypt. And went a-way!

Quiet! Quiet!

German Folksong

Qui-et qui-et make not an-y noise! Lis-ten lis-ten to the Ho-ly Voice! Won-der is now com-ing near, Je-sus Child is com-ing here. Qui-et qui-et make not an-y noise.

Spring Song

This song is made up completely in the pentatonic mood, with not even an inkling of tonic influences. Every phrase ends on that floating tone e, holding a question or a secret that is not abandoned. What would the tonic have to invoke indeed? A troll, a fairytale character, heavy, dumb and sleepy, does not give rise to the positive sound of the tonic. And the sunbeams which have to herald spring? They also produce that mysterious atmosphere of nature that five-tone music calls forth. The last phrase could have had a positive end on the tonic, but all the others—seven to be sure!—they end on $g - d - e$. In that case, it is too hard on a first grader to make a different end on the last phrase. That would ask for too much consciousness.

No need to say that this is a song to be play-acted. How gorgeous to scratch the troll on his nose, and…how difficult not to do so too early!

Spring Song

Text: Hermien Ijzerman
Translation: E.L.

Shepherd's Story

This song shows us the line of development we have followed in Grade 1. The text summarizes what we experience together in the "woodland meadow." The music descends from the fifth to the tonic including the semitone *e – f*. Of course we do not mention this; it is experienced unconsciously by the children anyway.

We have tried to keep the child's being in a clear and bright atmosphere in which gradually the tonic appears, little by little, emphasizing the child's feeling of living here and now in this, our world.

This song can also be played on the recorder as an exercise for alternating fingers on *e – f*. It is the same sort of descent as in "Frosty, Frosty Winter," but now in the diatonic sphere.

Comparing the two songs, one feels that in the "Shepherd's Story" the floating mood of five-tone music is missing. It is stating facts, and not only in the text! For us adults, that might be only a trifle, but for the children it means a lot!

✻ Shepherd's Story

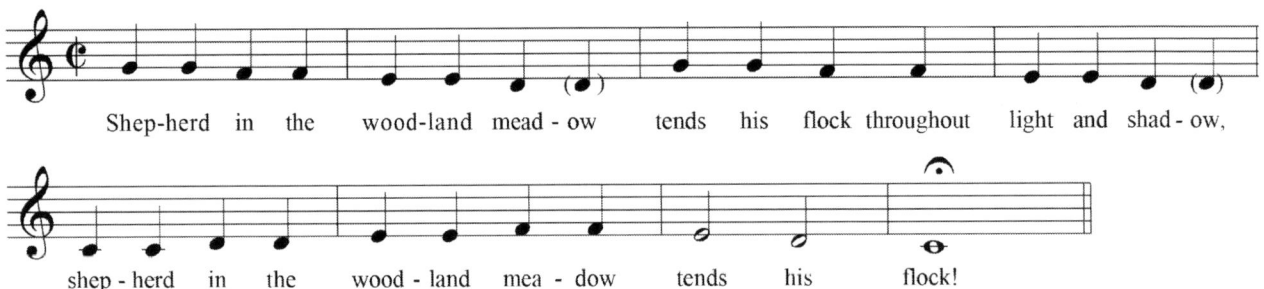

2. Sheep are grazing grass and clover
   Closely watched by faithful Rover,
   Sheep are grazing grass and clover
   Yes! They do!

3. Day is dark'ning, it gets cold!
   Sheep are going to the fold.
   Day is dark'ning, sheep are going
   To the fold!

4. In the fold they sleep all right
   Sheep and lambs throughout the night
   In the fold they sleep all right, good
   Night! Good night!

St. John's Song

In the Name of the Lord We're Riding

From *Das Brünnlein Singt und Saget*
Aloys Künstler. Translation: E.L.

✱ Sheep Shearing

Page 35

Notes:

Introduction to Grade 2

After the summer holidays it is always striking the way the former Grade 1 children appear in Grade 2. The dream world, in which everything wrapped in a picture "just happened," is gone! Evidently on their way to a tonic, very much conscious of each other's little habits, second graders often are in a squabbling mood.

On the one hand, one would like to go on in the five-tone mood (until the ninth year!), but on the other hand, the children are asking for a more outspoken musical language and, certainly, for a more outspoken end of a song. While in Grade 1, a song could end in the third or the fifth, as has been stated before, this is not accepted anymore by a Grade 2 child.

Now it would be wrong to conclude that this is the moment we may take leave of all that difficult pentatonic material with a sigh of relief and go right away into the more familiar sounds of well-known folksongs, into major and minor.

But in the course of history, major and minor did not result directly from the five-tone mood either. Pentatonics and major-minor are two extremes, and, in between those two extremes, we find just what second-graders need. We should be aware of the possibilities in between the two moods, that is: a pentatonic musical language with a more outspoken end (see folksongs from Scotland, Ireland, etc.—only, mind the texts!) and the old church modes that can provide us with a musical language that fits marvelously with Grade 2 consciousness.

Properly speaking, we never think of the fact that songs made up with the tones $c-d-e-f-g$ give us the feeling of being "here" and "now" in this world; we may experience them as naturally childlike but, compared with pentatonic songs, they have a totally different, much more earthly quality. Conditioned as we are to this sort of sound, it is very hard to gradually become aware of those subtle differences in musical mood—differences we should be able to work with.

The only fifth interval we are really familiar with is the one with the semitone between the third and the fourth tones. On whatever tone we might start this sequence, however many sharps or flats we might use, the sound of this sequence always gives us the feeling of "being home." If we take the sequence of the fifth $e-b$ however, in which the semitone is in between the first and the second tones, then all of a sudden we are far from home in our feeling. The c in the sequence $c-g$ has an outspoken tonic character, the e of the sequence $e-b$ is just hanging, the whole sound is floating, asking, calling!

Now we should try to experience this sound as such, apart from feelings of sympathy or antipathy, just as a phenomenon. To study the different ways to compose a fifth, in regard to the place of tones and semitones, one should consider the following very simple musical phrase:

The fifth *e – b* has been put into a rhythmical-musical form. One could try to permeate oneself with this sound (I). After that, one could listen to the second version (II). The semitone is now placed between the second and third tones. The whole atmosphere is changed! Going on in the same way, one could now bring the semitone between the third and the fourth tone … all of a sudden we are "home." The semitone between the fourth and the fifth makes the whole thing somewhat "strange" again! In this way one can become aware of the fact that, on the whole, one might have a long way to go to "unprejudiced listening"!

Here's another example in the pentatonic sphere. Searching for curriculum material for Grade 2 (fables), we might come upon the song of the cuckoo and the donkey, a simple German folksong consisting of the tones in the fifth *c – g*.

Harmonized it would sound like this:

Whoever listens accurately might hear in the second measure on the tone *f* a going inward, a receding, in any case a change which is also manifest in the chord by which it is accompanied. Two sounds, in this case two minor descending thirds, operate alternately, arousing different feelings (think of "Oats, Peas, Beans and Barley Grow" and so many others!). Although these sensations do not rise into conscious perception, one should not think such a thing has no effect! It is a duality that at this point in a child's musical education is not yet appropriate, although, as Rudolf Steiner remarks explicitly in *The Human Being's Experience of Tone*, it does not really do harm. Of course we cannot avoid this sort of song, but we should try to bring other material as well to establish a healthy balance.

To come back to the cuckoo and the donkey: We could give it a pentatonic costume and then the duality disappears right away, and also the inclination to provide it with chords. If we would want them anyway, it would sound like this:

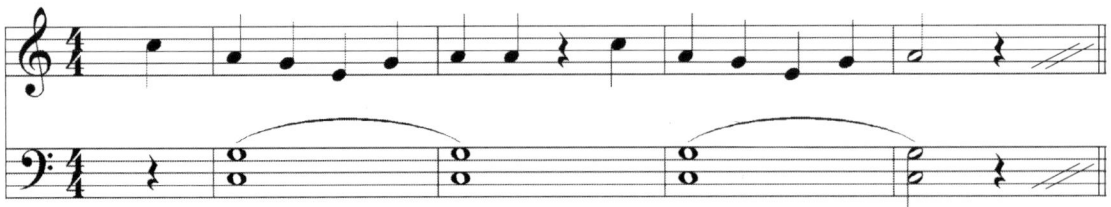

Page 38

Gone the duality! Everything is resting on the tone *c* as tonic. But this we can also eliminate by producing an accompaniment of the fifth *g – d*, and *a – e* appearing in their inversion as a fourth. The *e* over it gives a feeling of being "outside." The sharpness of these sounds is meant to express the not quite harmonious sounds of a cuckoo and a donkey.

In this way the feeling of a tonic disappears and everything is directed outside, an "outside" in which the second grader is still mainly living, although his feeling for the tonic is growing. That feeling should be supported as well. Scottish, Irish and other later pentatonic forms that have developed with people's consciousness, but not yet quite into major and minor, could do an excellent job here.

In the meantime we have to get on with recorder playing as well. In a way we start from the beginning but on a different level. No sing-song to start with! Now the three-tone songs (pages 23 and 38) can be played again, but not in a dream-like state. They should be really well known and everybody should be able to play them, individually, by heart. The songs with five tones can be managed in the same way. The C scale should now be built up systematically. By the end of the year, one should be able to play very simple material in that range, be it in a moderate tempo even, and more or less fluently.

For alternating fingering between *b* and *c* and between *e* and *f*, some exercises are given. Everything special for the recorder is again marked with an asterisk.

Verse

From: *Heilende Erziehung*
by Julia Bort, Natura Verlag Arlesheim

All things a-bout me I must love, and in-to me must take! The earth be-low, the sky a-bove, a part of me must make!

Jolly Nonsense

From: *Ga i Skoge*
by Hans Børre Ørbaek

Do come a-long! Do come a-long! Now let us sing this beau-ti-ful song, If we now sing this beau-ti-ful song, we may be sure we do get a-long! Li, li, li, lu, lu-re lu! Li, li-re li-re lu-re lu-re lu! Le, le, la, lo!

Nonsense Song

Harald Lyche & Co.
Music Publishers, Dramman, Norway

From: *Ga i Skoge*
by Hans Børre Ørbaek

Tu-re, lu-re, tu-re, lu-re! Teng, teng, tang! Peng, pin-ge, pang! Give us a birth-day cake, which we will glad-ly take! Tra-la-la-la-la! Tra-la-la-la-la!

Fall

Sum-mer's leav-ing, light is weav-ing, doo - doo - dood-le - deed-le-doo!

    2. Fall comes hither, plants do wither, doo, doo, doodle deedle doo!
    3. Birds are calling, leaves are falling, doo, doo, doodle deedle doo!
    4. Twigs are rustling, squirrels bustling, doo, doo, doodle deedle doo!
    5. Darkness threat'ning, Christmas beckoning, doo, doo, doodle deedle doo!
    6. Candle's shining, hope abiding, doo, doo, doodle deedle doo!

Song of Praise

    2. The birds, high up in tree-top, they sing and praise Your Name!
       And also the snake's hissing, you would not even blame!

    3. The fishes that are swimming, to You they are not mute,
       You're hearing all their voices, to You they all are good.

    4. And in the sun, before you, the gnats and flies advance,
       They too, though not beloved, do in Your honour dance.

    5. The Sun and Moon are setting and once again they rise,
       And in Your world of wonder, all's equal to Your Grace!

Considering the melodic line of the "Song of Praise," the minor third turns out to be mainly ascending. Whereas the descending minor third feels like an encompassing gesture (as in "The Tones," see Grade 1), the ascending minor third has more of an evocative effect. To you... to you!... Dear God!... etc. Apart from the experience from the lyrics, one might be aware of the striking difference between the descending and the ascending forms of this interval. The tones are the same, but the direction they take seems to decide about the feeling quality.

The Moon

The beautiful interludes for instruments in this song give the opportunity for percussion playing, indicated in the curriculum for Grade 2. If chime bars are available, only two bars are needed. From a metallophone, all the keys except *e* and *b* could be removed. The interlude looks simple enough, but for a second grader it is quite a task to perform this correctly and well in time. Of course he should hear it first, played on a lyre or a recorder. Exercise in listening!

Song of Praise

From: *Das Brünnlein Singt und Saget*
Aloys Künstler. Translation: E L.

The Moon (P. Dehmel)

Translation: Lyn Willwerth

From: *Das Brünnlein Singt und Saget*
Aloys Künstler. Translation: E L.

3. Lighter it grows steady, a platter she has ready
   With very finest silver-sand, she scatters over sea and land.

Squirrel Nib-Nab

This "fable in music" is built on two alternating moods: on the one hand the fall mood, when nature collects itself after summer's abundance; on the other hand, a careless little squirrel, still playing on in the mood of summer. In music these two moods are expressed respectively by the dorian scale ($d – e – f – g – a – b – c – d$) and by the D major scale ($d – e – f\# – g – a – b – c\# – d$).

To be able to sing this song, the teacher should master the dorian scale, both ascending and descending. In the sentence, "Leaves are turning red and gold," the dorian mood expresses itself characteristically. Compare this with, "O! Come now, it's not yet rough!" In the former we have $d – c – b – a$ descending, in the latter $d – c\# – b – a$, giving us a feeling of joy in the outer world.

When removing $c\#$ to c, all of a sudden we are in a different place! The flowers, the abundance of fruit, everything has gone! The birds, whose wing-strokes we experience in the 6/8 measure, try to bring Nib-Nab back to reality, but this obstinate little fellow answers again in the mood of summer: "Come now, birds…" But then, with three big steps ($f – g – a – b$), causing that strange, drawn-out atmosphere, November comes in! It's getting serious!

Now Nib-Nab has to gather food for the winter, and he's not in the jolly summer-mood. With the rhythm of the squirrel's first, lighthearted sentence, but now not in major, but in the dorian scale, the fable ends with the usual moral advice.

Squirrel Nib-Nab

Text: Brigit Visser

Page 45

Squirrel Nib-Nab (continued)

Das Wilde Tier

This song, for teaching the children to count in German, offers a unique chance to express two different moods in music. "We would like to go into the garden" (an open fifth), but.... that wild animal! The melody goes up to *g* and *a* but then takes a turn into four descending tones, arranged in the same way as the first four tones in C major.

This turn is the cause of the remarkable change of mood on: "Wenn nur das wilde Tier nicht käm'." When the wild animal finally appears, the whole C major scale, with the structure of the ascending form, now descends.

This mirroring of tones and semitones produces a very strong effect of which the teacher should be well aware. If not, the *d flat* at the end will no doubt come out as a *d*! Use a gong or another metal percussion instrument.

2. Die Glock' schlagt drei, die Glock' schlagt vier, das wilde Tier ist noch nicht hier.
3. Die Glock' schlagt fünf, die Glock' schlagt sechs, das wilde Tier ist wohl verhext!
4. Die Glock' schlagt sieb'n, die Glock' schlagt acht, das wilde Tier ist nun erwacht!

St. Martin

On the 11th of November, shortly after Halloween, it is St. Martin's day. The legend of St. Martin, who, to warm a poor beggar he finds on the roadside, divides his own cloak in two parts with his sword, might be told in the main lesson. Hopefully, this song will enliven the story.

St. Martin

English Lyrics: E. L.
© Bärenreiter Verlag

From *Heiligenlieder* by Walther Hensel
Bärenreiter Verlag, Kassel

He trav-els a - lone, St. Mar - tin, the Ho - ly St. Mar - tin!

    2. He's riding his horse, St. Martin, 'Long mountains and hills, St. Martin!
    3. On roadside sits an old, old man. "Please give me some warmth, St. Martin!"
    4. He take his cloak and cuts it in two, The Ho - - ly St. Martin!
    5. "I am not a poor and old, old man, Oh! Ho - - ly St. Martin!"
    6. "It's Me Myself, your own dear Lord, Oh! Ho - - ly St. Martin!"

Epiphany Song

After Christmas it is always a challenge to find the right material for the month of January. Though in this book many festival songs could not be included, this little "Epiphany Song," in the dorian mode, might be of some help in this situation.

The tiresome journey is expressed in the first sentence with the tones $d - e - f - g - a$, but the light appears with the tone b! If one should try to sing it with a *b flat*, what a difference!

Sweetest Childe

In former times, this old Dutch Epiphany song was sung by groups of children, who dressed up as the Three Kings with old tablecloths, crowns on their heads, stars on sticks, and went from farm to farm singing Christmas carols.

The text of this song may lead to some play acting: the Kings asking to be admitted, Mary answering. Mary, sitting on a bench, the Child in her arms, could be the Madonna, but she could also be the peasant's wife, welcoming the visitors. Thus the situation hovers between dream and reality.

The sentence: "'t Has been born" should be sung by the whole group. The song is made up in the dorian mood, the *b* again carrying the light.

✳ Epiphany Song

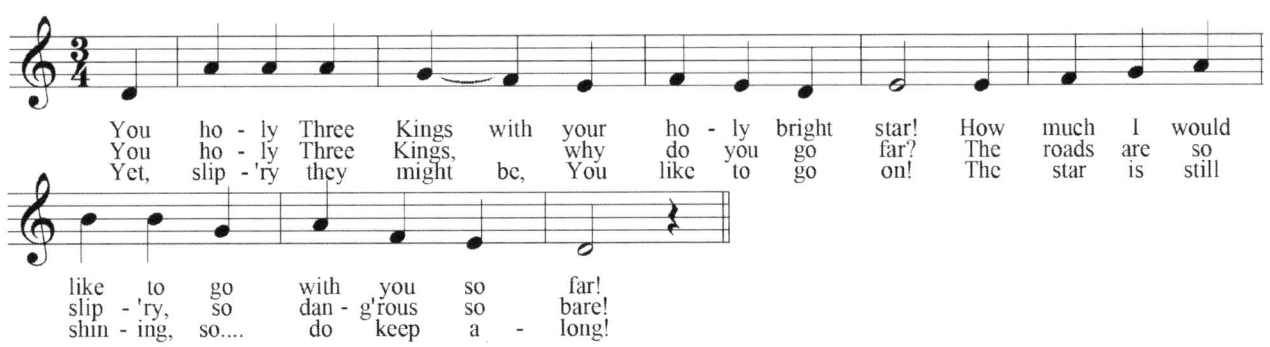

You ho-ly Three Kings with your ho-ly bright star! How much I would like to go with you so far!
You ho-ly Three Kings, why do you go far? The roads are so slip-'ry, so dan-g'rous so bare!
Yet, slip-'ry they might be, You like to go on! The star is still shin-ing, so.... do keep a - long!

Sweetest Childe

Dutch folksong

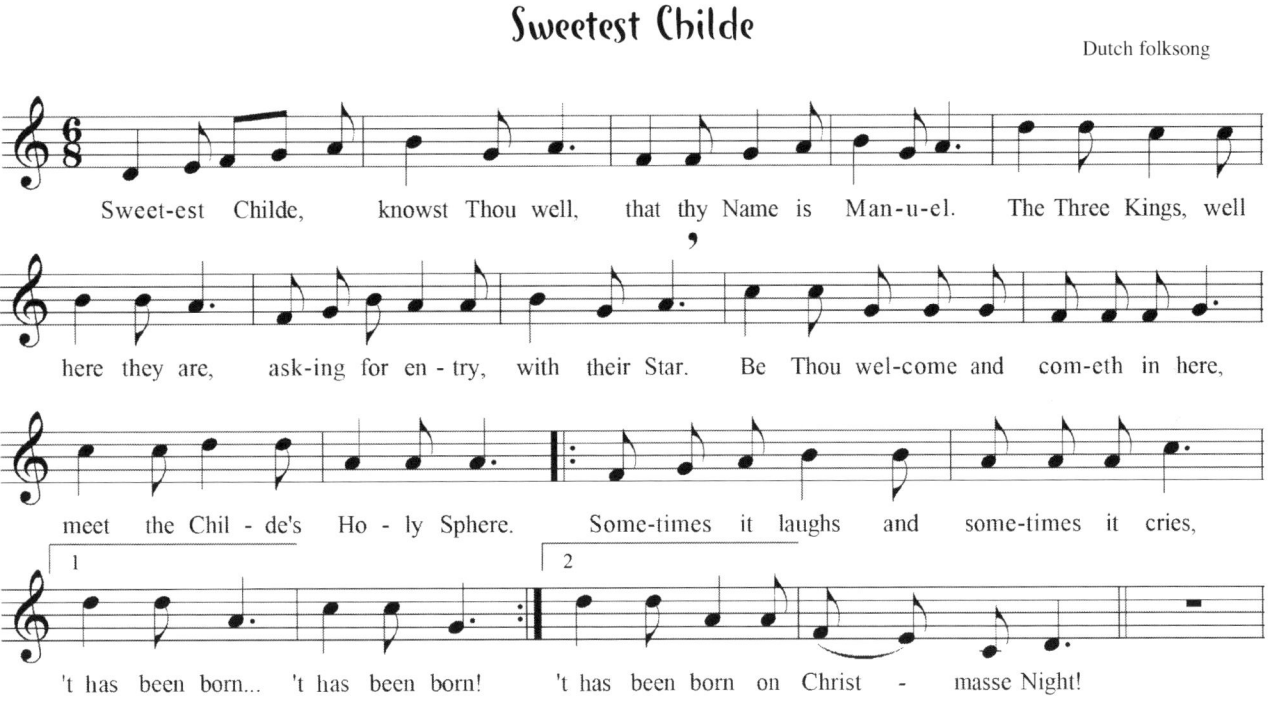

Sweet-est Childe, knowst Thou well, that thy Name is Man-u-el. The Three Kings, well here they are, ask-ing for en - try, with their Star. Be Thou wel-come and com-eth in here, meet the Chil - de's Ho - ly Sphere. Some-times it laughs and some-times it cries, 't has been born... 't has been born! 't has been born on Christ - masse Night!

✳ Round

When the swan sings: Doo-did-el-dieu! Doo-did-el-dieu! Doo-did-el-dieu!

Page 49

Songs with Five Tones

The Tortoise and the Hare

Text: Alan Howard

"O, where are you go - ing to?" said the hare to a tor-toise he met on the road.

"Crawl-ing like that, do you think you'll get there? you can't e - ven hop like a toad!"

Tor-toise said noth-ing but kept on his way, and the hare bound-ed off, full of pride. "I'll

tell them you're com - ing," he laughed, "one day! a pit - y you can't get a ride!"

Tor - toise said noth-ing, but kept on his way, and pres-ent-ly passed by the hare, who,

ti - red of run-ning, a - sleep on some hay, was dream-ing how fast he'd get there.

Tor- toise said noth- ing, still kept on his way, nor wast - ed a thought on the hare, who,

when he ar-rived at the end of the day, found the tor-toise, found the tor-toise,

was al - read - y was al - read - y, was al - read - y there!

Winterstreams

It will entirely depend on the mood in the classroom whether the children will enjoy singing this song or not. Perhaps a winter story could prepare them?

To illustrate the intimate atmosphere, the sharp winter air and light, one or more triangles could be used to join in with the slight tinkle of ice, the murmuring of the little bit of water that escaped from being frozen.

A sevenfold rhythm moves throughout the song, alternating four and three beats in every two measures. The triangles should play on the first and second beat of each second measure. This is indicated by the sign ∧.

Catalonian Christmas Song

This song, in the second part, should be accompanied by percussion, maybe by a whole choir of joyous sounds (preferably on metal) played on every beat. That seems to be very simple! However, in the first part there should be no percussion at all! Hence this is a concentration exercise, for if only one child forgets himself and plays too early, the whole unexpected outburst of joy on: "Ev'ry bird...," etc., is spoiled.

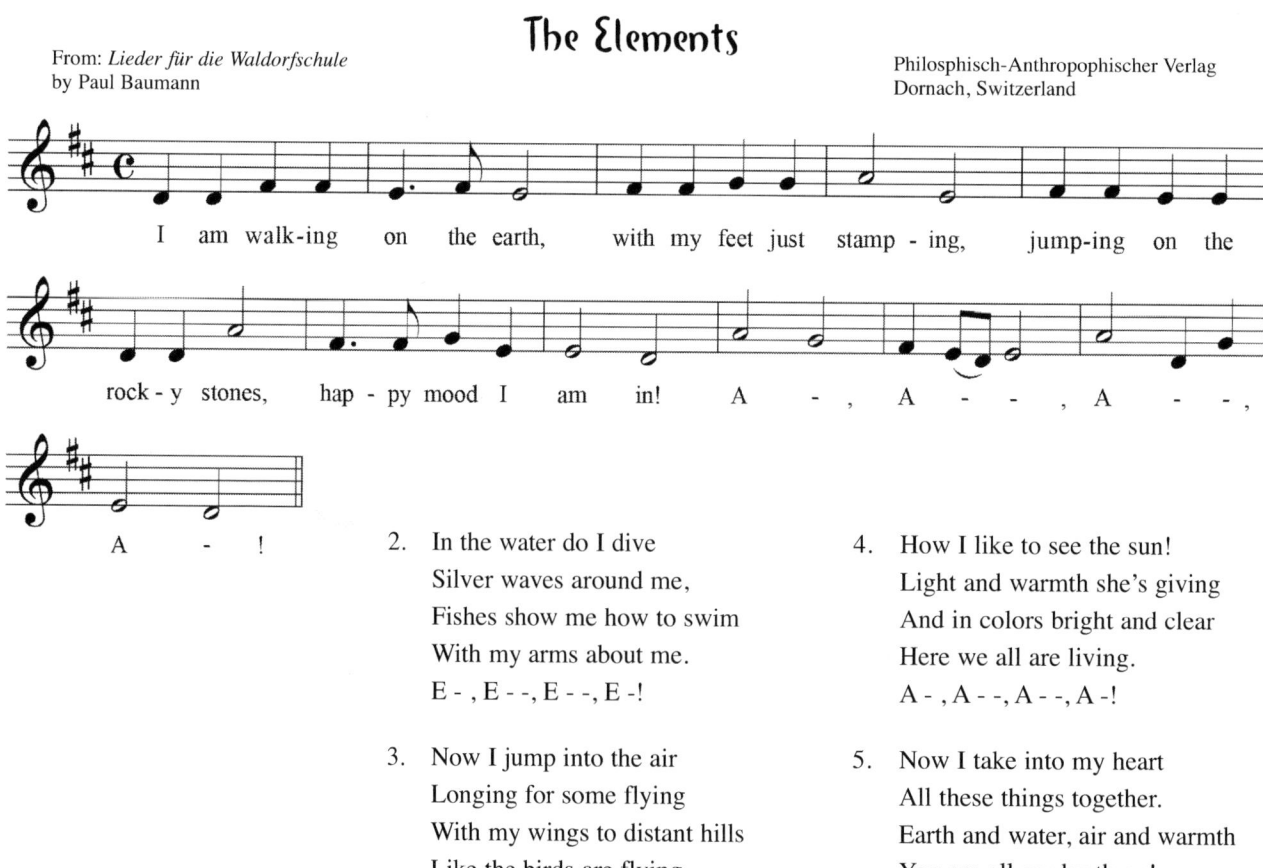

The Elements

From: *Lieder für die Waldorfschule* by Paul Baumann

Philosphisch-Anthropophischer Verlag
Dornach, Switzerland

I am walking on the earth, with my feet just stamp-ing, jump-ing on the rock-y stones, hap-py mood I am in! A -, A - -, A - -, A -!

2. In the water do I dive
   Silver waves around me,
   Fishes show me how to swim
   With my arms about me.
   E -, E - -, E - -, E -!

3. Now I jump into the air
   Longing for some flying
   With my wings to distant hills
   Like the birds are flying.
   I -, I - -, I - -, I -!

4. How I like to see the sun!
   Light and warmth she's giving
   And in colors bright and clear
   Here we all are living.
   A -, A - -, A - -, A -!

5. Now I take into my heart
   All these things together.
   Earth and water, air and warmth
   You are all my brethren!
   E -, E - -, E - -, E -!

Winterstreams

Reprinted by special permission of the
Bliss Carmen Trust, The University of New Brunswick

Text: Bliss Carmen

Catalonian Christmas Song

Folksong

Page 53

The Cuckoo and the Donkey

This song has already been mentioned in the introduction. The whole group sings verse 1, in verses 2 and 3, the cuckoo and the donkey have solo parts. The accompaniment can be played on lyre, metallophone or chimebars. This is a good exercise for three children who have to play their tones together and at the right moment. That means a good part of listening; the song starts with an upbeat, which they should not play! The end of the last verse is different from the end of verses 1 and 2.

2. The cuckoo said: "Just hear me!" and made a loud, "Cuckoo."
   But then the donkey joined him (2x), "Just hear what I can do!"

3. That sounds so nice and lovely from nearby and from far.
   They're singing both together (2x), "Cuckoo! I-A! cuckoo! I-A! cuckoo, cuckoo! I-A!"

Verse 3 ending

The Crow and the Fox

Text: Alan Howard

1. A crow, with some cheese, sat down at her ease to eat it up-on a high tree. A fox pass-ing by, who did this es-py, said: "That must be mine speed-i-ly."

2. "Oh! crow!" he exclaimed, "I'm really ashamed, I've never yet heard how you sing! When ev'rywhere round the praises resound of your beauteous voice in the spring!"

3. The crow, full of pride, at this opened her beak wide and cawed loudly and shrill: While fox, with a smile, rejoiced at his guile, and swallowed the cheese with a will.

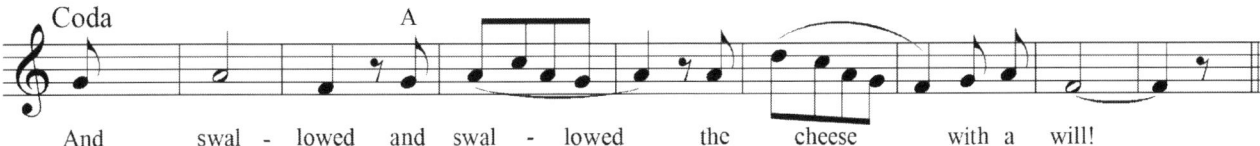

And swal-lowed and swal-lowed the cheese with a will!

Recorder Exercise 1

This exercise has been made up for alternating fingering on $b - c$. On the word 'happily" the fingers start "walking." The idea of Snow-white walking through the wood will be a great help for all those children who need a picture to guide them into activity. The song can also be played on $d - e - f$ as an exercise for alternating fingering on $e - f$.

✳ Recorder Exercise 1

In the sev-en moun-tains, near the sev-en foun-tains, dwarfs were liv-ing hap-pi-ly, loved their Snow-white well!

Page 55

April

At the end of the second year in school, it might be interesting to investigate the group's reaction to a pentatonic song of nature that does not end on the tonic. Will it be rejected? The tune is given a bright and active quality by ascending and descending fifths. It should not be sung too slowly, nor too heavily, but on the other hand not too fast! The accents in the text speak for themselves. The melisma at the end should be elaborately spun out.

Text: Christian Morgenstern
Translation: Lyn Willwerth

From: *Das Brünnlein Singt und Saget*
Aloys Künstler. Translation: E L.

2. We who now are walking
   Suddenly are breaking
   From the willow tree.
   Deepest dreams we're keeping,
   All the winter sleeping
   In the wood, you see!

3. In the dry, rough willow,
   On your tiny pillow
   Had you been asleep?
   In the hard wood sitting,
   You soft furry kittens,
   Did you dream too deep?

4. Understand our meaning
   What therein was dreaming
   Where we not yet quite
   As we now are showing
   Silk and velvet glowing
   In the sunshine bright.

5. Like what thoughts could render,
   Lay we in the slender
   Willow branches gray.
   Unseen spirits willed there
   Which the World's great Builder
   Therein did us lay.

6. Pussies in the willow,
   Like a downy pillow
   In your silken gray!
   Silver kittens hiding,
   Now I know you're biding,
   Know where you did stay.

Page 56

April

Text: Herien Ijzerman

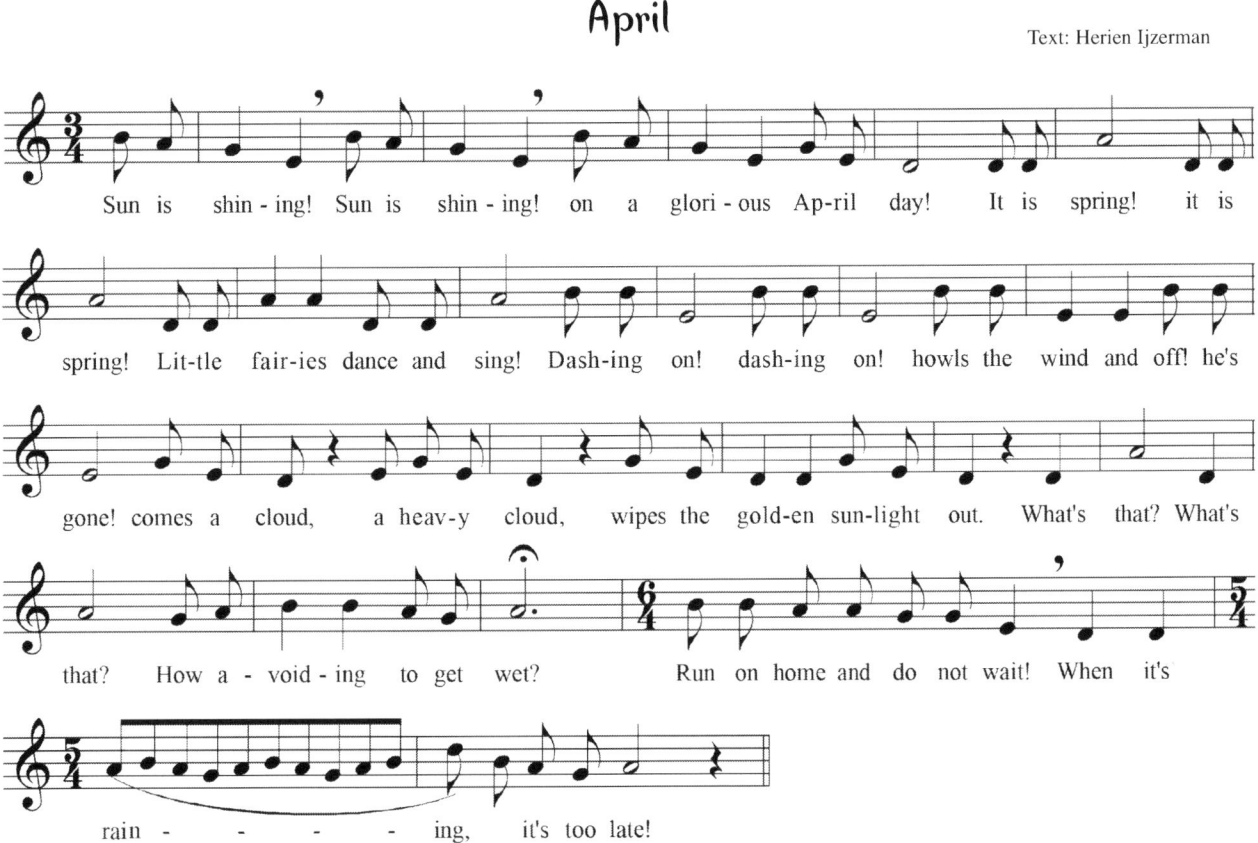

Recorder Exercise 2

This is a continuation of Recorder Exercise 1 on page 53. The tones are the same, only the alternating fingering on *b* and *c* is more frequent.

✱ Recorder Exercise 2

The Three Fables

The three fables can be a valuable contribution to the main lesson, during the time these stories are told. Each has a different rhythm.

In "The Crow and the Fox," the willing element is expressed in the repeated combination of iambus and anapest. (page 53)

In "The Tortoise and the Hare," the rhythm is more even, the difference between the two animals is expressed in the melody being more lively for the hare, followed by the unperturbed reaction of the tortoise. The last word: "There!" should be emphasized by a beat of cymbals. (page 49)

The humorous mood of "The Stork and the Fox" is expressed by the dancing rhythm going on until the victorious end, where it changes to an emphasized statement of triumph for the stork.

The dotted rhythms should not be sung too fast and should be accentuated correctly. No percussion!

Lullaby

"Lullaby" from Wales is a typical example of the pentatonic mood which in Scotland, Ireland and Wales still lives on in folksongs. The tonic is there, but the semitone is still lacking. The melody, though of the utmost simplicity (most of the song is made up of only three tones, not more!) has a very special inner quality of which "Now do sleep well, I pray" is the culmination. The tone *b* is first touched from below by *g* and *a*, after that from above by a descending third. A wonderful turn of phrase, full of secret life. One should really try to penetrate such a thing in a meditative way to be able to realise its depth. The song can also be played on the recorder.

The Stork and the Fox

Text: Alan Howard

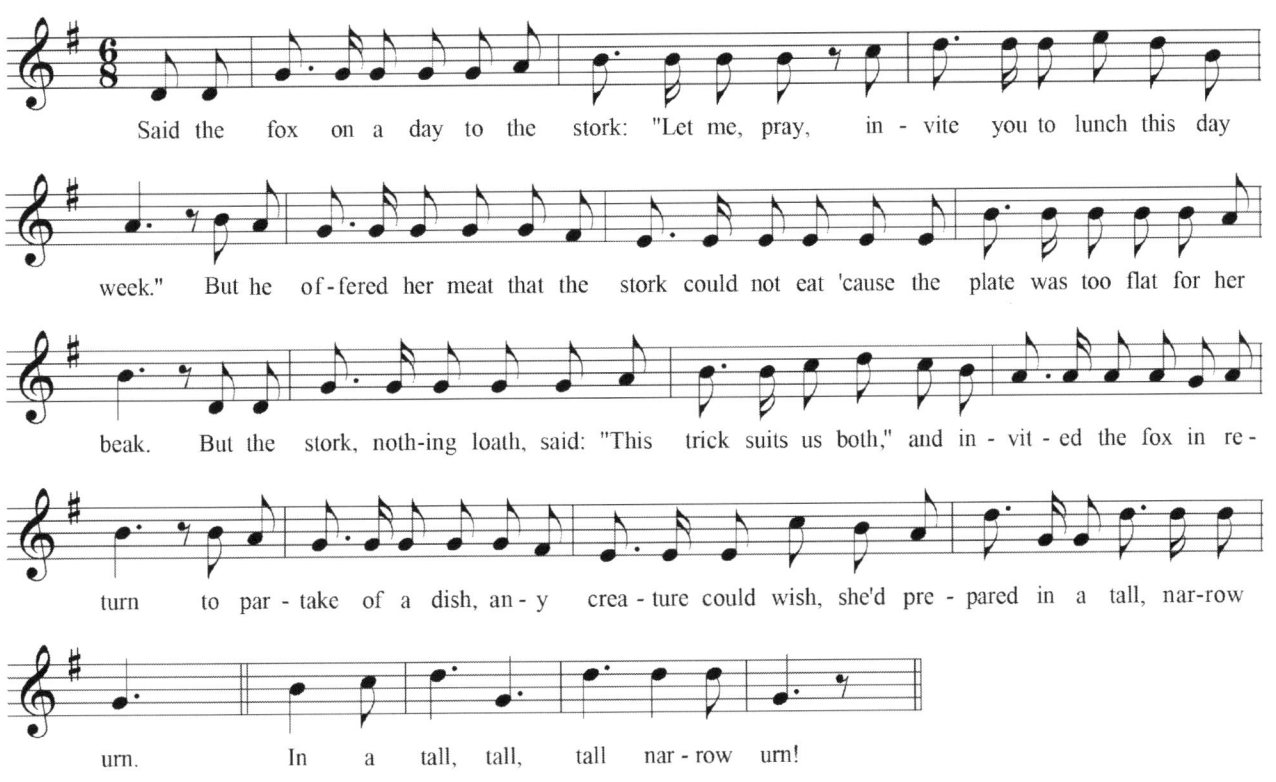

Said the fox on a day to the stork: "Let me, pray, in-vite you to lunch this day week." But he of-fered her meat that the stork could not eat 'cause the plate was too flat for her beak. But the stork, noth-ing loath, said: "This trick suits us both," and in-vit-ed the fox in re-turn to par-take of a dish, an-y crea-ture could wish, she'd pre-pared in a tall, nar-row urn. In a tall, tall, tall nar-row urn!

✳ Lullaby

From Wales

Su-ja-doo my ba-by good-night my love good-night. Su-ja-doo my ba-by, your moth-er's here all right! Now do sleep well, I pray! t'mor-row we will sing and play! Su-ja-doo my ba-by good-night my love, good-night!

Page 59

✳ More Songs with Five Tones

Fais Dodo

Oats, Peas, Beans and Barley Grow

May Song

J'ai du Bon Tabac

German Folksong

One, Two, Three, Four

Sweet Mary

Notes:

Introduction to Grade 3

Having worked mainly with the pentatonic scale in Grade 2, we now have to deal with quite different demands in Grade 3. In the course of this school year, third graders will be nine years old and thus will reach their tenth year, in which a very important change in their inner life will take place. Some of them might already be nine in October! We will have to see to it that this change of attitude will be given full attention also in music.

We are going to say goodbye to the pentatonic scale. At this stage, the religious mood of the old church modes can serve us well as a musical frame for the stories of the Old Testament. Any religious content that possibly can be given to third graders at this point in their lives, where "outside" is on the verge of becoming "inside," will be of great value.

The musical expression of that "outside" we experienced in the five-tone mood. The growing "inside" we feel in the church modes. This changes gradually into genuine major and minor experience, being the musical expression of individual soul life later on. But in Grade 3 we are not yet that far along! The nine-year-old has only just started to discover himself as separate from a world with, until now, he has been naturally united. His growing feeling of self is supported and nourished by the old Bible stories that speak of unity with and obedience to God. Preferably, musical material relating to this unity should be used.

In music, this is the moment we take the last steps toward the experience of the outer world in major and the small growing patch of inner world in minor. However, we do not yet alternate major and minor as distinctly as we will have to do in Grade 4. We just use these elements with as much consciousness as possible to support those feelings typical of third graders. The songs relating to the Old Testament will serve the development of the inner world, as was mentioned before, but, as in Grade 3 the trades are dealt with, one has the opportunity to bring quite a few "doing" songs in major: simple, sturdy demonstrations of the love of work. The ones presented in this book are only a few of the many possibilities. They are also good material for recorder playing.

In Grade 2, we tried to play on the recorder the whole of the C major scale plus *f sharp* and *b flat*, and, in a modest tempo, songs that had been sung first. This in Grade 3 has to be expanded. We will see that the group has already a certain awareness of what it is able to produce on the recorder and even a slight critical awareness. The children now usually want more and harder tasks. To meet this need, one can try to bring some instrumental pieces, and also the very simplest rounds (of which we include only a few as examples) can serve a profoundly felt need for "greater enterprise." Played in unison, these songs are considered "easy," but can be more challenging to sing and play them accurately as rounds. Much patience on the part of the teacher is needed to bring this process to a somewhat satisfactory end.

Until now the recorder has been played by heart with some visual help on the teacher's instrument. This, of course, cannot go on, and the children in Grade 3 will have to be taught musical notation. The way this can be done according to "Waldorf principles" will be described in a separate chapter. It should be started right away during one of the two weekly music sessions. This subject also meets the need for more difficult material. Often quite a few children are already dealing with musical notation in connection with playing an instrument. However, they rarely object to taking part in the exercises given here; on the contrary, these most often seem to be a welcome support to what is already being taught in a visual and haptic way.

Our way of teaching notation is a slow, gradual process based on the development of the sense of hearing. It does not claim completeness in any way. We try to bridge the abstract character of this new script with pictures and movements, just as we brought the alphabet letters in Grade 1. What do we have of all our efforts to work with the child's awakening intellectual forces in the right way if we just thrust him into musical notation? When abstraction is bridged by means of pictures and movements, there is time enough to proceed further in a more usual way.

In Grade 3 there is a lot of musical work to be done in recognition of the fact that, whereas until now music has served us, from now on we in turn will slowly but gradually learn to serve music with the best of our abilities.

Ohne Zahl

From: *Jung Horand*
Published by Wilhelm Dörffler Dornach

Him-mel-sau, licht und blau, wie-viel zäh - lst du Sterne? Oh - ne Zähl!

So-viel Mal sei ge-lobt der Got - tes Sohn!

2. Gottes Welt, wohl bestellt,   wieviel zählst du Staublein?
3. Sommerfeld, uns auch meld,   wieviel zählst du Halme?
4. Dunkler wald, grüngestalt,   wieviel zählst du Zweige?
5. Tiefes Meer, weit umher,   wieviel zählst du Tropfen?
6. Sonnenschein, klar und rein,   wieviel zählst du Funken?
7. Ewigkeit, lange Zeit,   wieviel zählst du Stunden?

God Is Good

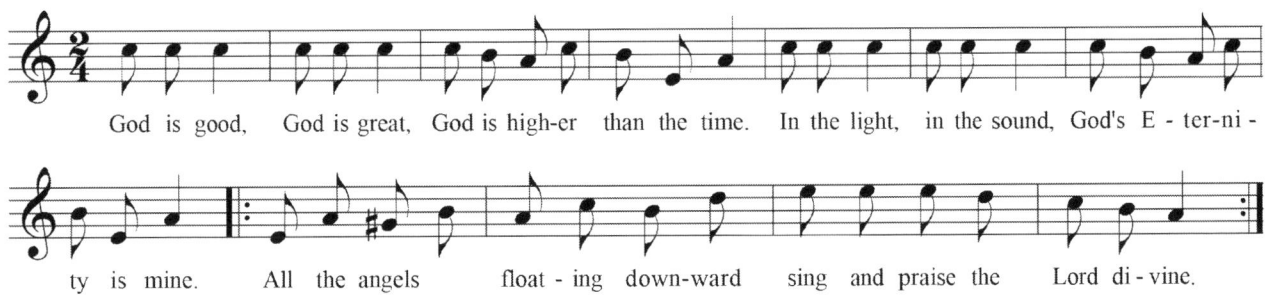

God is good, God is great, God is high-er than the time. In the light, in the sound, God's E-ter-ni-ty is mine. All the angels float-ing down-ward sing and praise the Lord di-vine.

✷ Advent Song

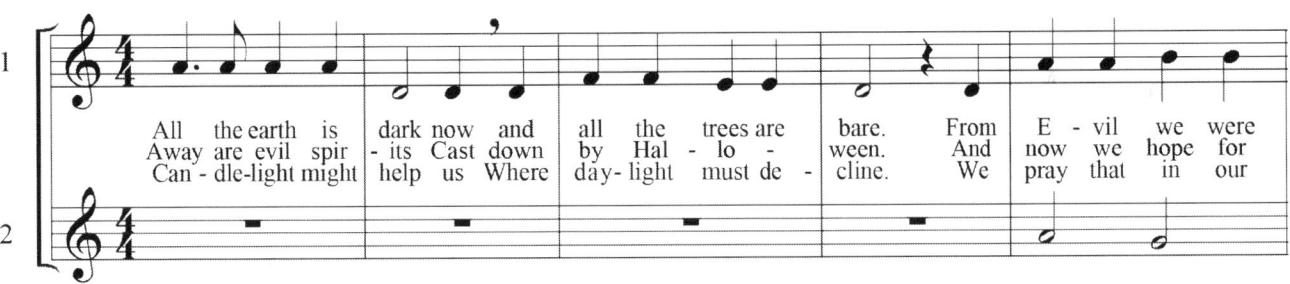

All the earth is dark now and all the trees are bare. From E-vil we were
Away are evil spir-its Cast down by Hal-lo-ween. And now we hope for
Can-dle-light might help us Where day-light must de-cline. We pray that in our

guard-ed by brave St. Mi-cha-el, by brave St. Mi-cha-el!
Ad-vent. Will in-ner light be seen? Will in-ner light be seen?
hearts and mood the Christmas light may shine! The Christ-mas light may shine!

Page 65

The Plumber

Dutch folksong

A - plumb-ing! A - plumb-ing! my ket-tle has a hole. It's the plumb-er who mends the ket-tle for us, that's to say: for ag-es it has been thus!

The Carpenters

Dutch folksong

1. The car-pen-ters' is the fin-est trade, a trade to be men-tioned with honour. What would have be-come of our dear old world if no-bod-y ev-er'd used a ham-mer? With-out the trade of the car-pen-ter oh! Man-kind no doubt would have per-ished long a-go.

2. Had Noah not been a good carpenter
   He could not have saved his kin at least.
   He worked with hammer and chisel and nail
   To built his ark for man and beast.
   Chorus: Without the trade of the carpenter...

3. A carpenter cherished Jesus our Lord
   When He'd just been born on that Holy Spot.
   St. Joseph protected the little Child
   Against the sword of cruel Herod.
   Chorus: Without the trade of the carpenter...

4. The carpenter makes a bed for himself,
   He makes a crib for his childe,
   He makes a coffin of six small boards,
   O, Lord, to his soul then be milde!
   Chorus: Without the trade of the carpenter...

2. O where, o where has that flour come from?
   You wouldn't know?
   Miller put grain between his millstones,
   Crushing it, grinding it fine and neat,
   The sweeps of the mill going fast,
   The wind is blowing full blast!

3. O where, o where has that golden grain come from?
   You wouldn't know?
   Farmer took millions of tiny seeds,
   Sowing them densely in waiting earth
   That had been prepared with manure,
   The grain coming forth to be sure.

4. O where, o where does that growing come from?
   You wouldn't know?
   Earth and Heaven, they work together:
   Heaven blessing with love and light,
   Thus the wind and the sun and the rain
   Do grow the golden grain.

Earth, I'm Aware of Thee

Text by unknown German author

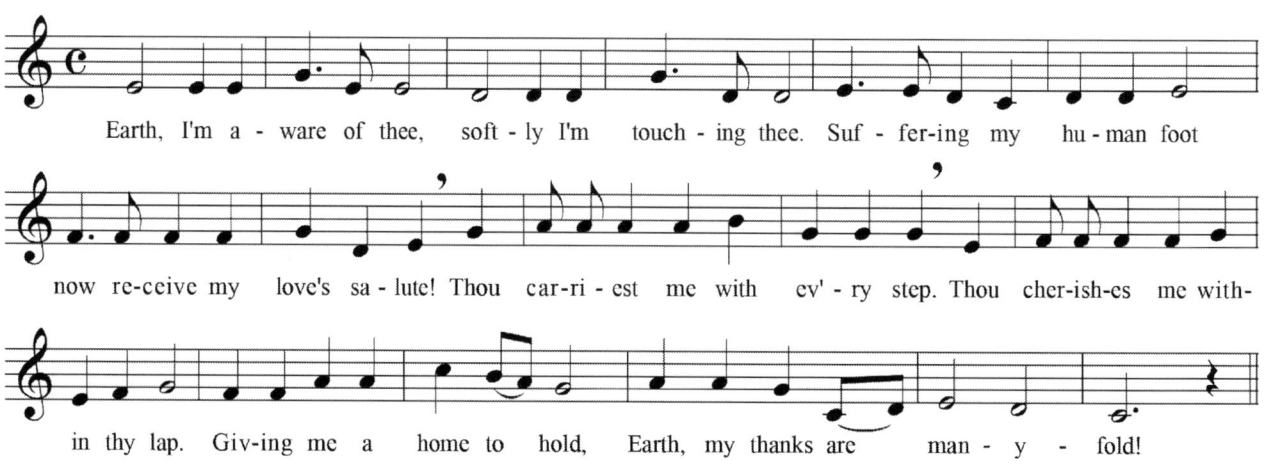

Earth, I'm a-ware of thee, soft-ly I'm touch-ing thee. Suf-fer-ing my hu-man foot now re-ceive my love's sa-lute! Thou car-ri-est me with ev'-ry step. Thou cher-ish-es me with-in thy lap. Giv-ing me a home to hold, Earth, my thanks are man-y-fold!

I Once Went on a Morning

Old Dutch

I once went on a morn-ing in-to the woods...., behold! And there I saw the mar-vels of God's Works man-i-fold! The birds were sing-ing and mak-ing noise, the rab-bits ran so free-ly, my heart was full of joy!

 Dance

* Bonsoir

The Water Mill

Forerunner Publications
England

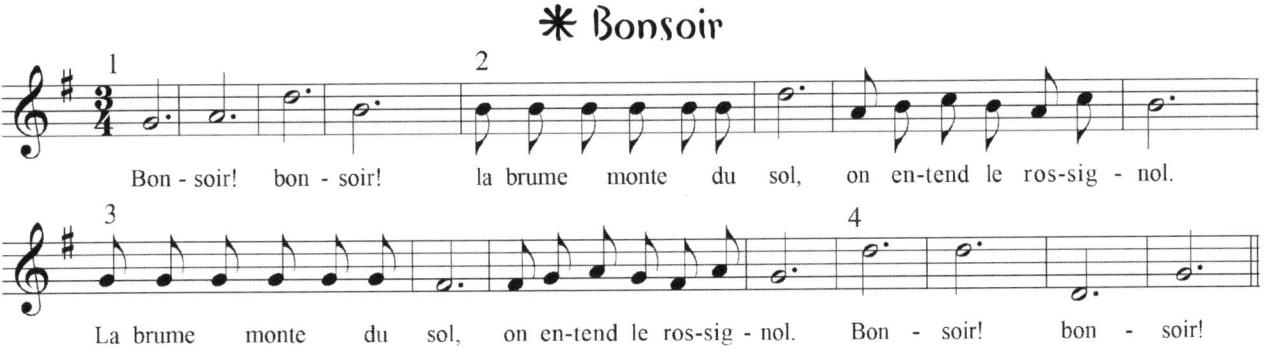

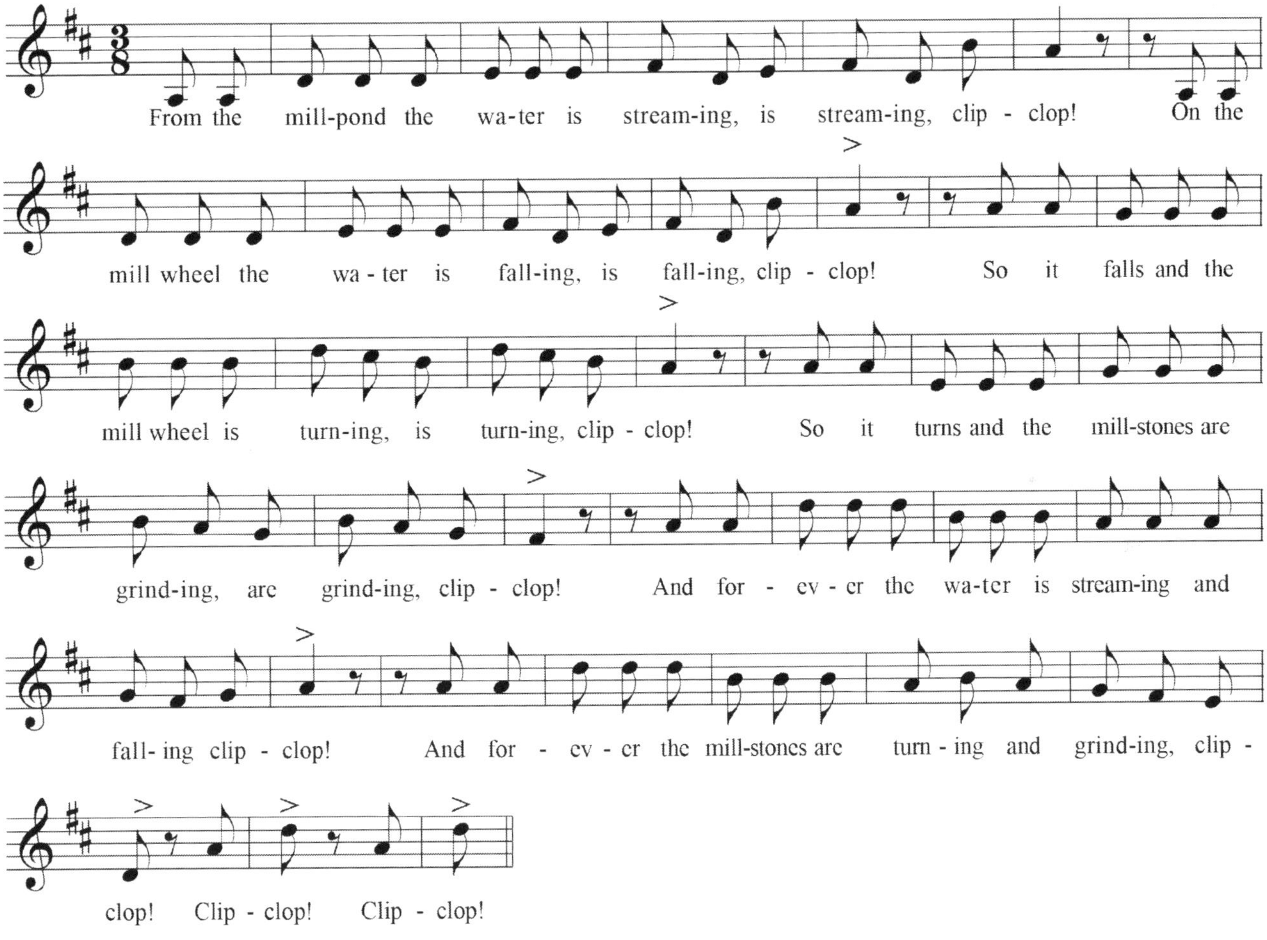

* Hiaderia

From: *Der Fünfton*
B. Schott's Söhne, Mainz

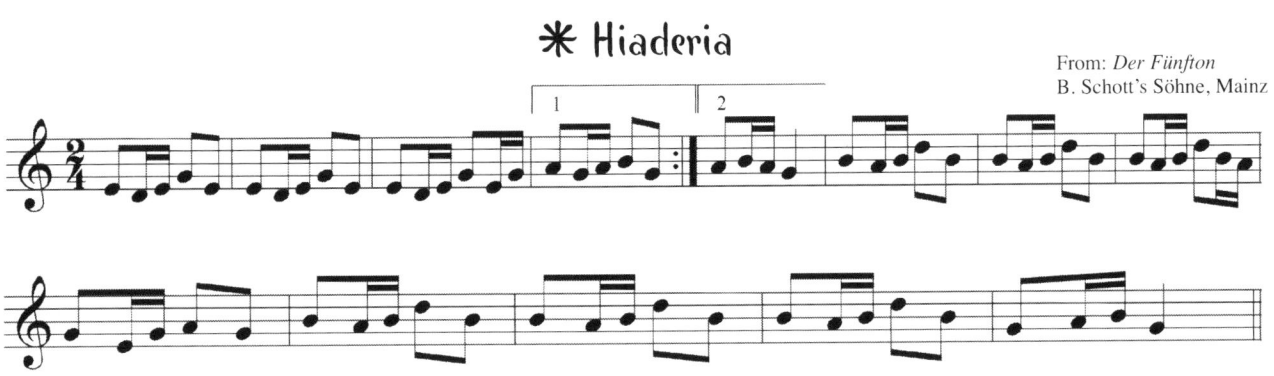

Who Can Tell Me?

Who can tell me what one does mean? Oj, wej, oj, what one does mean?
Whoever can tell me what one does mean?
What's the meaning of one? What's the meaning of one?
Chorus: Only God is one... and further there is none!

Who can tell me what two does mean? Oj, wej, oj....... etc.
Two mean the two stone tables, two mean the two stones tables
God alone is one!
Chorus: Only God is one... and further there is none!

Who can tell me what three does mean? Oj, wej, oj..... etc.
Three mean the three patriarchs, three mean the three patriarchs,
Two mean the two stone tables...
God alone is one!
Chorus: Only God is one... and further there is none!

Four mean the four mothers....
Five mean the books of Moses...
Six mean the books of Mischa...
Seven means the Holy Sabbath...

"Who Can Tell Me" is an excellent song for singing when, for whatever reason, there is some commotion going on in the group. The great length, the continuous repeating and the retrospective enumeration have a calming effect, whereas the song's sound rouses enthusiasm despite the minor scale. "Only God is one" solemnly lands in the tonic. The song is made up in original minor: a sequence from *a* to *a* without sharps or flats. Here it is transposed into the key of D. Again, it is the arrangement of tones and semitones which gives the special flavour, the specific character to such a sequence. One should try to sing the last sentence with a *c sharp*... and the whole flavour changes!

Ani Maǎmin

This song might not look too attractive to teachers! The difficult Hebrew text, the many dots and bows are not inviting! However, this song turns out to be most rewarding after the first obstacles have been mastered. The children marvel at the strange words and love to sing the melody. (See Introduction to Grade 3 about "typical feelings.")

For the Hebrew pronunciation, some expert help may be needed. The song is made up in original minor, with a minor sixth, in this case resulting in a *b flat*. In the first measure on the third line, this *b flat* becomes *b*. This is a dorian tune, producing the same sort of light effect which we experienced in the "Epiphany Song" of Grade 2. The *b*'s in measures 5 and 7 do not have that quality because in those sentences *a* is tonic, hence the *b*'s have a different function. In measure 9 the melody goes back into D minor again.

Who Can Tell Me?

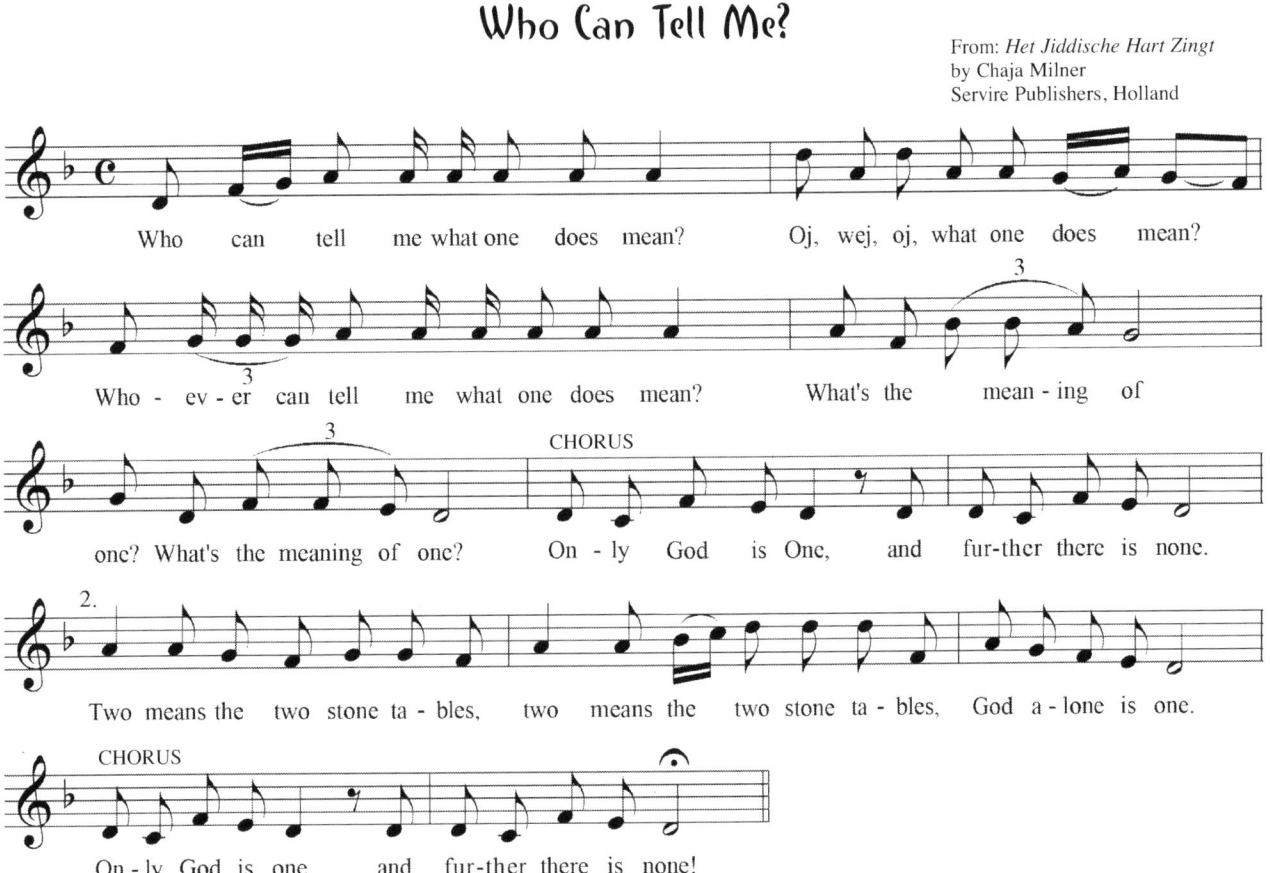

Ani Maämin

Kol Dodie

From: *Hoor de Stem van Beminde*
by Chaja Milner
Servire Publications, Holland

Kol Dod-ie, Kol Dod-ie, Kol Do-die hi néhzèhba. Me-dâ-lég'-al hé-ha-riem - me-ka péts 'al ha-gewa-'ot, me-da-lég 'al hé-ha-riem me-ka-péts 'al - hagewa-ot.

Psalm 150

Psalm 150 is made up in a very free rhythm. The text has so many accents that the melody just cannot be caught in a continuous measure nor in note values. One should not feel obliged to count or sing the triplets too exactly: They are only meant to speed up the text, to give a certain emphasis to the words. One should be inspired, carried on by the evocative character of the psalm.

The melody is mixolydian—that means a sequence from *g* to *g* without sharps or flats. Transposed into D it gives the following scale: $d - e - f\# - g - a - b - d - d$. This sequence ought to be studied in its own character, not as a D major scale without $c\#$.

The greatest difficulty in the first line is the $f\#$ on "praise." The descending $c - a$ on "sanctuary" often inspires the children to make a downward triad to *f*. However, if this song is presented well by the teacher without hesitation (and that means with conviction) at some time every day during a week, there will be no trouble.

Psalm

Although made up in the same mixolydian sequence, this song could not be more different from the former one. Here the text is secondary to beat, which might be emphasized in the rests between the phrases by percussion, exclusively on metal. Also very unconventional instruments like a piece of copper curtain rod pierced at the top, hanging on thin iron wire, and played with a long heavy nail can serve. The more tinkling, the better! The rests should first be counted, then clapped (counting inwardly) and finally played on the percussion instruments. Most often the attention of many children is so diverted by the instrument in their hands that this way of proceeding is not quite unwarranted.

✳ Round

Morn-ing has come, night is a-way, rise with the sun and wel-come the day!

Page 72

Psalm 150

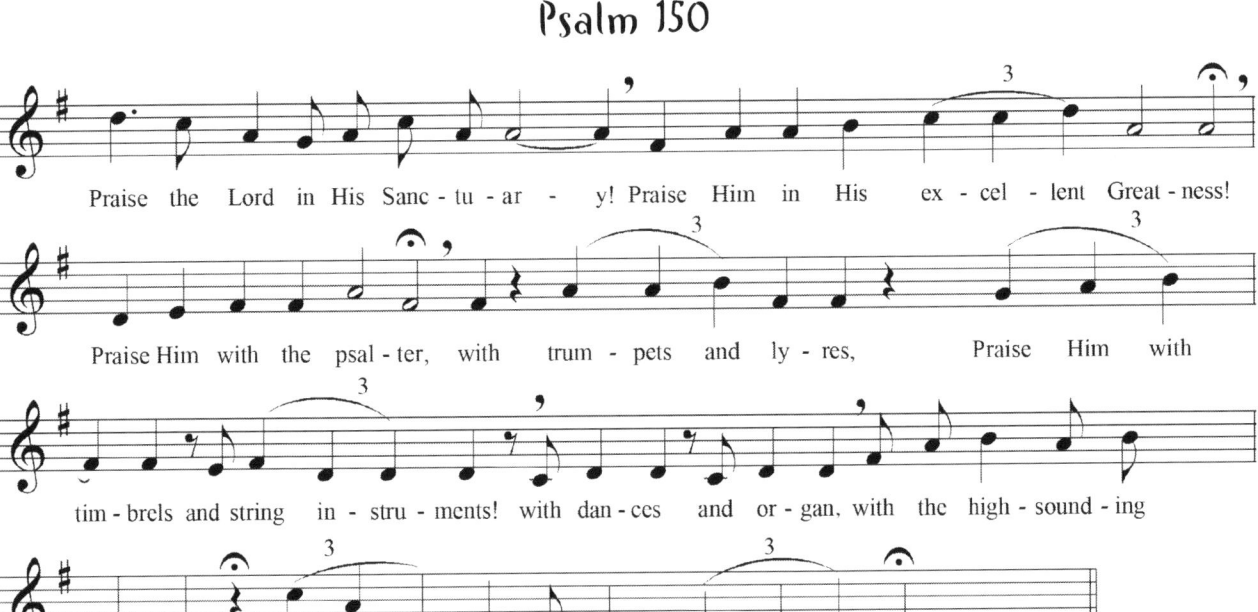

Psalm

Musical Notation

The teaching of musical notation should have a special place in the music lessons in Grade 3. This script, presenting oval shapes on lines with stems, hooks and dots, is even more abstract than that of the alphabet letters whose signs at least have their own identity. But in musical notation, one note looks exactly like the other, their identity only recognized by the place they take on the five lines of a musical staff.

In many cases, children are confronted with musical notation the moment they start playing an instrument. The notes are presented in connection with a certain key on the piano, with covering holes on the recorder or finger placements on string instruments. The players on the latter are well off! They at least have to listen to the tones they produce. But the pianists and recorder players experience the tones they are producing as a result of the movements they make, which in turn are brought about by an act of seeing. In this way, there is scarcely any activity of the sense of hearing.

For that reason we choose not to use an instrument for teaching musical notation but start from active hearing. This certainly will take more time, but what would prevent us from proceeding step by step in as lively and pictorial a way as we can manage? Let us try to make a scheme of stages that we will go through to put oval shapes, representing the tones, on five lines in such a way that the child's imagination is fully engaged and involved.

Rhythm

As "rhythm was in the beginning," we should start with longer and shorter notes. It makes no sense to tell the children: Look! this is a quarter note, it is solid and takes one beat (what is a beat?) and that is a half note, it is hollow and takes two beats, so it is longer! These are statements which do not appeal to the child's imagination. We should avoid speaking of "beat," but rather we *do* "beat" by clapping, stamping and tapping the different note values of a well-known song and then write it down in a notebook (blank pages, please!) on a single line. For example, the first of the three-tone songs on page on page 38 will looks like this:

In this way the experience of a simple rhythm goes from hearing and feeling through limb activity to a primitive concept of rhythmic script.

Pitch

This stage is considerably harder to handle. As the real music occurs in the intervals, not in the tones themselves, the melodic *line* in its movement might be the very first step into an awareness of "higher" and "lower." For this the group in the classroom could move from left to right singing a simple song and "writing" the line of the melody in the air. (A delicious moment when "the line is up" and everybody runs back to the left to start a new one!) This can be written in the notebook and decorated with motives of the song's text. It is quite amazing what children can produce in this respect.

This is what was made of a German "Jack-o-lantern" song:

Laterne! Laterne! Sonne, Mond und Sterne! Brenne auf mein Licht!

Of course after some time we all feel this is too vague, and the tones should now be located. We can do this by means of a picture representing a river, a road or a brook, drawn on the blackboard. This provides us with three areas in which we can put signs according to the song.

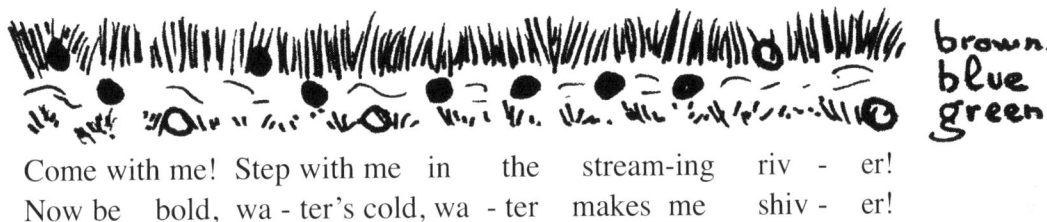

Come with me! Step with me in the stream-ing riv - er!
Now be bold, wa - ter's cold, wa - ter makes me shiv - er!

In this picture we have three areas, a "reed" area, a "water" area and a "meadow" area: brown, blue and green. This picture can be drawn in the notebook. It could also be drawn on the floor so that the song can be "walked" in it.

Then we can draw two lines in the notebook (hitherto non-abstractly represented by the banks of the river!) and colouring them blue in between to represent the water, and do the same thing as was done in movement: writing steps, prints or tracks above, in between and below the two lines, according to the song. This still comes very close to what we would like to avoid: just seeing the notes and making the appropriate movements, although we did it the other way round: hearing and then taking the appropriate steps.

We still need another stage of limb activity in order to establish a real feeling for "higher" and "lower." For this one could have a wooden staff made: two vertical poles with holes at the distance of a child's fist through which five wooden sticks can be fitted in. This provides us with a staff, showing the notes on the lines, but which can be grasped by the child. The notes "in between" can be experienced by the child's fist which is literally *in between*. Such a staff also has the advantage that as many sticks (lines) as are needed can be put in. In this way we are able to produce our three-tone songs on this staff with the child's own living hand, on the basis of hearing. (Do not try to make cardboard notes or the like to hang, the notes should be invisible!

Gradually we will come to songs with more than three tones, but do not go on in this way too long because the notes, being dead oval shapes, only get their identity by the place they have on the five-line staff. That is why the children should now have a picture of a whole staff and find out how many notes can be put on it naturally: five "line" notes, lying on the staff, and four "in-between" notes, hanging from the staff. Naturally this whole procedure is followed by writing down in the notebook everything that has been experienced and practiced on the wooden staff. Now the children can fill the whole staff with the eleven notes.

That might seem quite easy, but usually it turns out to be the opposite. Many children have trouble putting the notes on and between the lines properly.

Once the notes can be located on the staff, they should be given names. Again the *a – b – c* for the oval shapes on lines is not too inspired a way to deal with them! Why not have an *a – b – c* family with the children's name? The seven letters are usually represented in the group—if not with first, then with last names. That makes working with these letters much more lively—quite a different experience! The different members of the family now have to take their places on the staff. If a hall is available, the family of tones could be brought in one by one from a distance while the group sings:

Afterward, those whose name are not in the *a – b – c* family should carry their friends' tones to the appropriate place. The teacher's imagination might find many games to play in this situation.

The last thing to do is to fix the names at their places by the clef. The *g* person is the lucky one. The clef keeps the secret where the tones' places really are. Imagine *a* suddenly wanting to have a different place! The whole family would have to move! Therefore *g* says, "I'm on the second line from below, and there I'll stay and you'd better keep in line!" And he fixes a beautiful golden clef on the staff. The clef's form could also be drawn on the floor and walked by the children singing:

Round about and up and down,
With a little curl close to the ground.
It's the *g*, his house and hall,
Or treble-clef as it is called.

This might be the right place to ask ourselves why the notes have not been presented by the relative, the do – re – mi names, which would also open up the possibility of illustrating the mobility of clefs. Apart from being a rather difficult concept for third graders, it is also a question of principle.

In Grade 3 there is still a feeling for essence, for quality. In introducing the tones in notation to our students, we should find a way to present them as different beings. Of course we cannot involve planets or signs of the Zodiac. However, by linking the note names to those of the children, we direct their attention to quality. This feeling for quality in our time, in which quantity seems to rule, is in danger of getting lost. The relative names of notes belong to functions in the scale and can be applied to any tone and do not express anything about that special tone's being. These names can serve the teaching of scales in the higher grades. If the quality of the tones has been well experienced in Grade 3, then the quality of a major scale in D or F will also be experienced as being different from that in G or C.

There is a strong tendency toward conformity in the world, that is to say, to value quantity over quality. In olden times it was just the opposite: The qualities of tones and even of numbers were experienced naturally, so that Pythagoras' arithmetical investigations into music were something quite new. We could try to recapture this old feeling for quality by presenting the tones as beings—in our case in the form of human beings. For example, present the *a* as this special being "Ann." She could also be "do," the tonic of a scale, just as "Ann" can be "mother" or "daughter." Those are functions in which the being of "Ann" is living. But the beginning, the kernel, is "Ann." The tonic as "do" can unfold its sequence, the seven tones of the diatonic scale, at twelve different places. Here the seven planets and the twelve signs of the Zodiac appear in their mutual musical relations (see *Art in the Light...*, page 90, ff.) The human being appears on earth as an individuality in a special place (of the Zodiac = 12), functioning in the hereditary stream (in time = 7).

See Rudolf Steiner: *The East in the Light of the West*, lecture 9.

It might seem far-fetched to link the ideas mentioned here to teaching musical notation. But it's necessary to be aware of what it is expressing. We have to do with tremendous realities. To express something of these realities in our teaching methods, especially with something as abstract as musical notation, might be one of our tasks as Waldorf teachers.

Contents

Preface to the New Edition 2023	5
Preface to the 2004 Edition	7
Acknowledgements	8
Preface 1975	9

Grade 1

Introduction to Grade 1	10
The Shepherd	15
Shepherd's Breakfast	15
Fox, Fox!	15
Gate into Recorder Playing	17
The Flock	17
The Tones	17
The Werewolf	19
The Squirrel	19
Rickydouse	21
We Dwarfs Are Working Happily	21
March Wind	23
The Song of Four Seasons	23
My Pony	24
Three French Two-Tone Songs	25
Kettle, Boil!	26
Sun Was Shining	27
Evergrace	27
Thawing	28
Sun and Rain	28
Cat and Mouse	29
Christmas Song	31
Epiphany Song	31
Quiet! Quiet!	31
Spring Song	33
Shepherd's Story	34
St. John's Song	35
In the Name of the Lord We're Riding	35
Sheep Shearing	35

Grade 2

Introduction to Grade 2	37
Three-Tone Songs	40
Verse	41
Jolly Nonsense	41
Nonsense Song	41
Fall	42
Song of Praise	43
The Moon	43
Squirrel Nib-Nab	45
Das Wilde Tier	47
St. Martin	48
Epiphany Song	49
Sweetest Childe	49
Round	49
Songs with Five Tones	50
The Tortoise and the Hare	51
The Elements	52
Winterstreams	53
Catalonian Christmas Song	53
The Cuckoo and the Donkey	54
The Crow and the Fox	55
Recorder Exercise 1	55
Pussies on the Willow	56
April	57
Recorder Exercise 2	57
The Stork and the Fox	59
Lullaby	59
More Songs with Five Tones	60

Grade 3

Introduction to Grade 3	63
Ohne Zahl	64
God Is Good	65
Advent Song	65
The Plumber	66
The Carpenters	66
The Blacksmith	67
The Bread	67
Earth, I'm Aware of Thee	68
I Once Went on a Morning	68
Dance	68
Bonsoir	69
The Water Mill	69
Hiaderia	69
Who Can Tell Me?	71
Ani Maämin	71
Kol Dodie	72
Round	72
Psalm 150	73
Psalm	73
Musical Notation, Rhythm, Pitch	74